# PERVERSION OF INDIA'S POLITICAL PARLANCE

# PERVERSION OF INDIA'S POLITICAL PARLANCE

SITA RAM GOEL

VOICE OF INDIA
New Delhi

First published: 1984
Revised Reprint: 1995
Second Reprint: 2009
Fourth Reprint: 2017

ISBN 978-81-85990-25-5

Published by Voice of India, 2/18, Ansari Road, New Delhi – 110 002 and printed at Replika Press Pvt. Ltd.

# Contents

# 1

# Something Seriously Wrong Somewhere

It was the summer of 1959. I was working as secretary of an organisation of which the late Shri Jayaprakash Narayan (J.P.) was the president. One day an RSS leader walked into my office. I had known him for a number of years. After some small talk, he suggested that I should request J.P. to visit an RSS camp which was being held in New Delhi at that time. J.P. also happened to be in town. I was diffident about the proposition. Having worked with J.P. for more than an year, I had sensed his preferences and prejudices. But I said to the RSS leader that I would do my best.

I broached the subject to J.P. next day as soon as I found him alone, which was a rare event. J.P. seemed to be stunned as if I had uttered an obscenity. There was an expression of disapproval on his face which made me too feel uncomfortable. He was a gentle person who seldom lost his temper. But now he seemed to be on the verge of exploding. The atmosphere became tense. For a few moments none of us could find words to break the spell of silence.

At last J.P. controlled himself and said, "Do you know what you are talking about, and to whom?" There was a touch of temper in his voice.

By now I had also managed to collect my wits to a certain extent. I said, "I knew that the proposition would be annoying to you. Even so, I took a chance."

He relaxed. I also heaved a sigh of relief. He said, "You know that I have a certain standing in the country and a certain reputation in public life. You should not expect me to get mixed up with an organisation which is known for its communal, reactionary, and revivalist character."

I said, "It is precisely because of your standing in the country and your reputation in public life that I have conveyed their invitation to you."

He said, "I do not understand. Could you make yourself a little more clear ?"

I explained, "Your standing in the country is that of a man of reason, and your reputation rests upon the keenness of your moral sense. I am sure your will live upto that standard in this instance as well."

He said, "I try to do my best according to my understanding and strength of will. Tell me where and how I have failed."

This encouraged me, and I said, "You have been practising untouchability towards a section of your own people. You have never met the RSS people face to face. You have never listened to their side of the story. Yet you have formed an unsavoury opinion about them. This does not sound reasonable to me, nor just."

He became thoughtful. I continued, "Your status today is not that of a party politician seeking power, and fomenting partisan strife. You have become a father figure for the nation as a whole, almost the conscience-keeper of our people. You raise your voice whenever you feel that an injustice has been done, or that justice is being denied. That is why people of all persuasions — Congressites, Socialists, Communists, Akalis, National Conference people, and who not — come to you for consultation, for registering their complaints, for presenting their point of view, and for seeking you advice. You do not always agree with them. Yet you listen to them patiently, and give them your point of view. They do not always agree with your view of men and matters, nor always follow your advice. The point is that you are always accessible to them. You always go out and meet them whenever they invite you. It is only the RSS and allied people whom you avoid, so much so that one of their leaders could not come to you directly and had to convey an invitation through a small fry like myself. Tell me if this is not tantamount to practising untouchability."

He closed his eyes and shook his head several times. He seemed to be engaged in some inner struggle. I pressed the point, "I am not inviting you to get mixed up with the RSS. Nor is it their intention to spread some snare for you. What they expect from a man like you is that you should try to know them first-hand rather than through hearsay or gossip in a partisan press controlled almost entirely by people who are hostile to them. Maybe you find that you have been mistaken about them. Maybe they benefit from the advice that you give them. But all this can happen only when you meet them, listen to what they have to say, tell them frankly what you feel about them, and thus open the door for a fruitful dialogue in days to come. In any case, heavens are not going to fall simply because you go and visit one of their camps. That is all I have to say. Rest is for you to decide."

He opened his eyes, smiled somewhat sadly, and said, "You have put me in a rather awkward position. But I can see the point in what you have said. I cannot easily refute your accusation. I can really be held guilty of practising untouchability."

I kept quiet and waited for him to make up his mind. He did it in a moment, and said, "Okay, you win. I am willing to visit the RSS camp. Make an appointment with them, and let me know. I hope tomorrow evening will suit them. Day after I am leaving Delhi."

Next day he spent nearly two hours in the RSS camp, witnessing their mass drill, moved by their songs of devotion to the motherland, meeting and talking to their leaders, asking all sorts of questions, and offering his own comments. Finally, he sat on a chair facing a group of about a hundred RSS workers from several parts of the country. The workers who sat on the ground in row after row, stood up one by one to introduce themselves to their honoured guest of the evening. Each one of them told his name without mentioning any surname indicative of caste or community, his educational qualifications, the province from which he came, and the years he had spent as a *swayaṁsevaka.* I could see that J.P. was impressed. His face which had been grim so far softened suddenly, and visibly. Most of the *swayaṁsevakas* held graduate and postgraduate degrees in arts, or commerce, or science. All of them were between the ages of 20 and 35.

At the end, J.P. was requested to say a few words, and bless the young men. That he politely refused. He whispered to me that he was quite confused, and did not really know what to say. I conveyed his feelings to the RSS leader who showed immediate understanding and did not press him any more.

As he was taking leave, J.P. looked at the *Bhagvā Dhvaja,* and observed, "That I suppose is the Maratha flag."

The RSS leader explained, "The Marathas did not invent it. They borrowed it from an age-old national tradition. The saffron colour has always been the colour par excellence of Indian spirituality as well as of Indian nationalism."

J.P. said, "I do not know. I have not been a student of history. But that is what a well-known historian told me."

The RSS leader smiled, and remained silent. The parting was rather warm on both sides.

On our way back, J.P. muttered as if he was talking to himself, "They have a lot of young and disciplined workers. Their workers are also highly educated. I never knew that. In our socialist movement, most of our workers are not even matriculates."

I kept quiet and waited for him to say something more. He made one more comment as we got out of the car at the end of our journey. He said, "Sitaramji, I am grateful to you for helping me break down what looked like an insurmountable wall. But I am not at all satisfied that it is not an attempt to revive the Maratha empire."

I could have asked him as to what was wrong with the Maratha empire. I could have also told him that the Maratha empire represented the triumph of a tough and long-drawn-out struggle against Islamic imperialism. But I was not prepared for some more frowns on his face. I had no status as a historian. Nor was my version of Indian history being taught in school and college text-books. J.P. was repeating what most of our historians were saying from their august seats in universities and research institutes. According to the professors, the Mughal Empire was a many-splendoured national mansion, while the Maratha Confederacy was a motley crowd of self-seeking marauders, out to disturb public peace and prevent the progress of national integration. How could I raise a controversy about what had come to be universally accepted in the world of learning? I was not even a school teacher.

## WHY I HAVE TOLD THIS STORY

I have told this story not as a part of my autobiography but in order to point out the gulf which divided a national leader from a national movement. Here was a leader who had fought for national freedom, and who was actively thinking and experimenting with methods of national reconstruction. And here was a national movement which took its birth at a critical juncture in the same fight for national freedom, and which was now concentrating on training our youth for the same task of national revitalization. Yet the two of them — the national leader and the national movement — stood miles apart, and could not see eye to eye on matters of major importance in national life.

Nor have I chosen J.P. simply because I happened to know him, and see him functioning from close quarters at one time. I have chosen him because he was a leader who had continued to grow out of closed ideologies, who had shed many prized prejudices, and who was sincerely in search of a wider vision. He was not like Pandit Jawaharlal Nehru and many others whose thought-processes became fossilized in the 'thirties or the 'forties, and who had subsequently failed to have a fresh look at national or international affairs. It was all right for J.P. to disown, even denounce the RSS so long as he was an orthodox socialist with his moorings in Marxist thought. But the event I have described took place several years after he had publicly renounced Marxism, and affirmed his faith in the path shown by Mahatma Gandhi.

Nor yet is it my intention to build a case for the RSS which is quite capable of looking after itself. I have chosen the RSS as the symbol of an ancient society and culture which have suffered for a long time, and in no small measure, from successive waves of aggressive imperialism let loose by Islam and Christianity, Capitalism and Communism. The aggression from all these dark forces is still continuing. There are many people like myself who have never been a part of the RSS but who nevertheless feel strongly that imperialist aggression should stop, that our people should come into their own in their ancient homeland, and that our culture should flower and make its characteristic contribution to the greater good of mankind.

J.P. had at last visited an RSS camp. He had been positively impressed by the quality of the workers whom the RSS had mobilized in the service of the nation. And yet he had retained his earlier reservations about the RSS. He could not visualise that the RSS was not a miracle which had materialized out of thin air. He could not see that there must be something in a society and a culture and a historical tradition which had created such a splendid band of selfless workers without the benefit of any patronage from the powers that be, and in the face of much malicious propaganda in the national and the international media.

These were some of the thoughts which arose in my mind at that time. I felt very strongly that there was something seriously wrong somewhere. But I could not resolve the contradiction. I failed to lay my finger on the sore spot in that sorry situation.

Ever since then I have pondered over the problem And I have at last come to a conclusion which I can now present with some confidence.

## POWER OF A POLITICAL PARLANCE

To my mind, the key to an understanding of the whole situation is to be found in the political parlance which has been prevalent in this country since the second decade of this century. Over the years, this parlance has been maligning the RSS as a "rightist, reactionary, and revivalist movement of militant Hindu communalism". Over the years, this parlance has been pillorying Hindu society as a "crowd of caste-ridden, cow-worshipping, and superstitious primitives". Over the years, this parlance has been ridiculing Hindu culture as a "close preserve of Brahmanism and some other forms of obnoxious obscurantism". Most of this mud has got stuck to the RSS as well as to Hindu society because neither the RSS nor the Hindu society at large has thought it fit to put up a defence, not to speak of turning the tables on the vicious adversaries.

J.P. was not the only one who had swallowed heavy doses of this political parlance in his younger days in India and abroad. There are so many others who have done the same in schools and colleges, in seminars and conferences, in discussions and debates. For, this pernicious parlance has been and is still being dished out on a large scale in most of the academia and the media, and in all other avenues of education, all over the country.

J.P. had at least tried to disgorge this poison, and succeeded to some extent in the later years of his life. There are many others who do not even suspect that they are being fed on poison, not to speak of making an effort to disgorge the doses which they have already swallowed.

I am not referring to those who have consciously chosen to be inspired by Christianity, or Islam, or Communism, or Consumerism, and who are thus committed to be hostile towards every effort at strengthening Hindu society and culture as a means to strengthening the nation. They are the hawkers of this poison, and find the profession very profitable. My reference here is to that Hindu intelligentsia who see a lot that is valuable in Hindu culture, but who run away when it comes to the defence of the society which serves as the vehicle of that culture, or who join the hawkers of poison whenever they find that this society is not going to take it any more.

I have done some investigation into the history and role of this political parlance which has by now become stereotyped into a series of mindless slogans. Today everyone is shouting these slogans, back and forth. But I fear that there are not many people, not at least in the political field, who have tried to find out the source of these slogans or the character of causes they serve.

I, therefore, feel emboldened to present my investigation in the chapters that follow.

# 2

# Words Which Defy Dictionaries

As one surveys India's political parlance, the first feature one notices is that while certain people and parties are described as Leftist, certain others are designated as Rightist. Once in a while, political scientists and journalists add nuances to this broad bracketing when they pronounce some splinter group as Left or Right of the Centre. But one is left guessing about the location of the Centre itself. It is sometimes suggested that the Centre is constituted by the ruling Congress Party. The Congress Party, however, repudiates this description.

The second feature which invites attention is that these contradistinctive labels — Leftist and Rightist — have never been apportioned among people and parties concerned by an impartial tribunal like, say, the Election Commission. What has happened is that certain people and parties have appropriated one label — Leftist — for themselves, and reserved the other label — Rightist — for their opponents, without permission from or prior consultation with the latter.

The third feature which one discovers very soon is that people and parties who call themselves Leftist, also claim to be progressive, revolutionary, socialist, secularist, and democratic. At the same time, they accuse the "Rightists" of being reactionary, revivalist, capitalist, and fascist. At this stage, the labels cease to be merely descriptive. They become laudatory and denunciatory as well. Labels like progressive and revolutionary etc., acquire an aura of virtue and holiness. On the other hand, labels like reactionary and revivalist etc., start smelling of vice and sin.

The fourth feature of the Indian political scene needs a somewhat deeper look because it goes beyond the merely political and borders on the philosophical. The Leftists claim that they are committed to a scientific interpretation of the world-process including economic, social, political, and cultural developments, and that, therefore, their plans and programmes are not only pertinent but also profitable for the modern age. Simultaneously, they accuse that the "Rightists" are addicted to an obscurantist view of the same world-process and, therefore, to such outmoded forms of economy, polity, and culture as are bound to be injurious at this stage of human history.

Lastly, one finds that the Leftists in general are pretty self-righteous as if some supreme power which presides over the world-process has not only entrusted them with the destiny of the Indian people but also assured them of an ultimate and inevitable victory. At the same time, the Leftists expect the "Rightists" to feel sorry for themselves as if the latter have committed or are out to commit some heinous crimes against humanity and, therefore, should not have any future except the dustbin of history.

It would be an interesting investigation to look up the dictionary meanings of these words which are being bandied around by the Leftists as political labels, and see if they really stick where they have been made to stick. Human history has known many instances in which the wolf has prowled and preyed in sheep's clothing, while the poor sheep has been presented as a wolf by sheer trick of language. The secularist version of medieval India under Muslim rule, as taught in our schools and colleges at present, is a case in point. Predatory invaders and mass murderers are being portrayed as illustrious emperors, while patriots and freedom fighters are being pilloried as local and petty upstarts.

On 13 August 1934, Pandit Nehru had written to Mahatma Gandhi that socialism had "a clearly defined meaning in the English language". The Mahatma had written back, "I have looked up the dictionary meaning of socialism. It takes me no further than where I was before I read the definition. What will you have me to read to know its full contents?"[1]

The various words which the Leftists now employ in order to applaud themselves and denigrate those who differ with them, can be found in any standard dictionary of the English language. But the dictionaries do not vouchsafe for the values with which the Leftists load these words. In most cases, the dictionaries assume prior definitions derived from different universes of discourse.

## LEFTIST VERSUS RIGHTIST

Dictionaries define a Leftist as "the more progressive or actively innovating party or wing (from its sitting in some legislature to the president's left)". The same dictionaries define a Rightist as "an adherent of the political right (conservative)". Neither of these definitions is

1. Cited by Sankar Ghosh, *Socialism and Communism in India*, Bombay, 1971, p. 183

very illuminating unless we have prior notions of "progressive" and "conservative". Nor are the values attached to these words evident in these definitions.

We shall discuss the word "progressive" when we come to it slightly later. Right now we can take up the word "conservative". The dictionaries define it as "tending or having power to keep entire, to retain, to preserve" and also as "averse of change". There is nothing intrinsically wrong with "keeping entire, retaining and preserving" unless it has been proved first that what is being kept entire, retained and preserved is undesirable. Nor does an "aversion to change" need be bad in itself unless the change that is being sought to be brought about has already been proved to be desirable.

### PROGRESSIVE VERSUS REACTIONARY

This second pair of labels is generally used to cover segments of socio-political opinion which are quite often broader than those covered by the first pair, that is, Leftist and Rightist. There are many people who do not relish being called Leftists. But they feel flattered when they are proclaimed to be progressives. Similarly, there are many people who do not mind being called Rightists. But they take fright as soon as they are called reactionaries. Leftist politics makes a cleaver use of this confusion. It ropes in as progressives many of those people who are not prepared to be known as Leftists. At the same time, it scares away or silences many people by branding them as reactionaries.

Dictionaries define a "progressive" as one who is "moving forward, making progress". That sounds tautological unless we have fixed some prior meaning of "moving forward" or have some prior notion of "making progress". The Leftists cannot get away with this label for themselves unless it is assumed arbitrarily that whatever they do or advocate should automatically pass for progress. Nor is it easy to arrive at a universally agreed definition of progress, particularly at the present time when all nineteenth century notions of progress are being subjected to serious questioning.

On the other hand, the dictionaries define a "reactionary" as "one who attempts to revert to past political conditions". This is a very vague and inadequate generalisation. Firstly, it is very difficult, almost impossible, for any people, at any stage of history, to revert to past political conditions unless those conditions are confined to quite narrow limits such as, for instance, the restoration of a royal dynasty. In fact, the word "reactionary" was used exactly in this sense during the French Revolution. Secondly, the past happens to be a rather long stretch of time in the history of most nations. It is not at all clear as to which part — ancient or medieval or modern — of a nation's past is implied in this definition. Thirdly, we cannot deride all attempts to revert to the past unless we assume arbitrarily that the past of all peoples was always worse than their present.

## REVOLUTIONARY VERSUS REVIVALIST

This third pair of labels is very weighty indeed. The very sound of the word "revolution" casts such a magic spell on our intelligentsia that many a time plain criminals draw applause from otherwise decent people by claiming to be revolutionaries. People who abhor their violence feel obliged to approve of them as "misguided idealists". No one has any tears to shed for the victims of these criminals masquerading as revolutionaries. The mangled bodies of policemen and other people are shoved away as unfortunate but unavoidable by-products of an unjust socio-political system.

The dictionaries define revolution as "a great upheaval; great change, i.e. in outlook, social habits and circumstances; a radical change in government". It is nowhere indicated in this definition that this great upheaval, this great change in outlook, social habits and circumstances, or this radical change in government is necessarily and invariably bound to be for the better. Even if it is for the worse, it will still be regarded as a revolution. Human history has known several upheavals which have left the people affected in an infinitely worse situation. The Christian revolution in Rome, the Islamic revolution in Arabia, and the Bolshevik revolution in Russia are outstanding examples of free people being brought under totalitarian tyranny. It may be psychologically satisfying for some people to press for a great upheaval, a great change, a radical change in government. But that is no reason for them to feel superior and self-righteous unless they can prove that they are working for a fuller freedom of man, for a greater measure of social prosperity, for a deeper culture of the human soul, and for a larger fraternity among different sections of mankind.

On the other hand, the dictionaries define a "revivalist" as "one who promotes religious, architectural or other revival". Obviously, the Leftists cannot be aiming their guns at architectural revival. Their objection has always been to religious revival. Religion has always been an anathema to the Leftists. This is understandable when we look at closed creeds like Christianity and Islam which strike at the very roots of rationalism, humanism and universalism, and extinguish all forms of human freedom except the freedom to convert or kill those who subscribe to a different belief system. But the objection becomes blind when it comes to the religions of the ancient world of which the sole survivor today is the commonwealth of Sanātana Dharma. They ought to distinguish between deeper drives of the human spirit from the fervour and fanaticism of the outer mind of man. And their ignorance in this matter is no reason for a blanket blackening of all religious revival.

## SOCIALIST VERSUS CAPITALIST

This fourth pair of labels arouses intense emotions. Socialism, too, is a magic word which paralyses all thinking processes in a majority of our politically conscious intelligentsia. It calls for no questions and stands self-proved. There is no political party in India which does not swear by Socialism. Ever since the ruling Congress Party has espoused Socialism, the socialist ranks have become swollen with a large number of self-seekers who cannot even spell the word. Seeing these people, one cannot help observing that while all socialists are not scoundrels, all scoundrels are socialists.

The dictionaries define "socialism" as "a scheme of social organisation which places means of production in the hands of the community". The same dictionaries define "capitalism" as "the economic system which generates and gives power to capitalists". Here the choice is clear for all those who place public weal above private profit. They would always vote for Socialism. The problem arises when the community is equated with the state, and the state with a monolithic party machine which chokes out all individual initiative and freedom. And that is exactly what the Leftists have done. They hail as socialist only those countries where totalitarian states have reduced the communities to conglomerations of dumb-driven slaves. In India, the Leftists describe the public sector as a signpost of Socialism. But this is merely a euphemism for a cartel of corrupt politicians, self-satisfied bureaucrats, and swollen-headed *bābūs* who are bribed and/or bamboozled by another cartel of freebooters known as the private sector. The two cartels fatten together with utter disregard for the suffering and privation they inflict on the community.

On the other hand, the Leftists denounce as capitalist precisely those countries where powerful labour unions, free press, parliamentary institutions, and vigilant public opinion have combined to make private enterprise accountable to the community. The rising standards of wages and consumption, the social security measures, and other welfare schemes speak volumes about how public good is gaining ground over private greed. The meaning of Socialism as well as Capitalism would have been crystal clear but for the conceptual swindle practised by the Leftists. They have succeeded eminently in painting the black as white and the white as black.

### SECULAR VERSUS COMMUNAL

This fifth pair of labels has attained the widest currency of all political words that are used in India. We face a peculiar problem here. The meanings which these words have acquired in India's political parlance are not even remotely related to the meanings which the dictionaries assign to them. It would not be an exaggeration to say that although these two words belong to the English language, their meanings in India are exactly the opposite of what dictionaries of the English language assign to them.

The word "secular" is defined in the dictionaries as "the belief that the state, morals, education, etc. should be independent of religion". But in India it means only one thing — eschewing everything Hindu and espousing everything Islamic.

Everyone who wants to qualify as secular in this country has to subscribe to the following articles of faith: 1) the Muslims in India after independence have become a poor and persecuted minority; 2) they are being deprived of their fair share in the fruits of development; 3) their religion and culture are not getting legitimate expression in public life and the media; 4) they are not being given employment in public and private sectors in proportion to their population; and 5) the preponderance of Hindus in the security forces puts in grave peril the lives, honour and properties of Muslims.

Every Hindu politician or pen-pusher who aspires to pass the test has to 1) proclaim that Islam stands for social equality and human brotherhood; 2) celebrate the Prophet's birthday with fanfare and throw an *iftār* party at the end of Ramzan; 3) attend *urs* of Sufis and Urdu *mushāirās;* 4) support the claim of Urdu to be the second state language in all states where Muslims are in a minority; 5) admire whatever passes for Islamic art and architecture; 6) relish Muslim cooking and appreciate Muslim dress and demeanour; 7) abuse Israel and applaud Arab countries.

He should also keep quiet or look the other way when Muslims 1) do not practise family planning and breed like rats; 2) refuse to give modern education to their children; 3) push their women into purdah; 4) practise polygamy; 5) start street-riots on the slightest pretext; 6) rejoice over every Pakistani victory and every Indian defeat in sports; and 7) invite and protect infiltrators and terrorists from across the borders.

And he should not whisper a word when Islamic states abroad pour petro-dollars into this country in order to equip professional preachers and practitioners of *jihād* so that this *Dār al-harb* gets converted into a *Dār al-Islām*..

Even these positive services rendered to Islam are not sufficient for a Hindu politician or pen-pusher who is out to earn the secular certificate. One is not secular unless one harbours a deep-seated anti-Hindu animus and expresses it quite frequently. One should lodge an immediate protest against the least little expression of Hindu religion or culture in public life and the mass media. One should frown upon every government dignitary performing a *pūjā* in a Hindu temple or going to a Hindu place of pilgrimage. One should accuse all educational, cultural and research institutions of hiding Hindu communalists. One should put the blame squarely on the RSS for every street riot. And so on, the list of one's grievances against Hindu society should be as long as one's love for Islam and Muslims.

The Indian definition of communal is a logical corollary of the above definition of secular. The dictionaries define the word "communal" as "pertaining to a community, owned in common, shared". But Hindus in India have only to say that they belong to a community, and that they share a culture in common; they immediately provoke secularists of all hues to come down upon them. In fact, the word "Hindu" itself has become a dirty word, almost an obscenity in India's political parlance. Woe betide the Hindu who dares say that India is his ancient homeland, and that his religion and culture also have a case. He will be immediately denounced as a Hindu chauvinist. A Hindu who blunders into reading Indian history with his own eyes, who finds that his society and culture have suffered immeasurably at the hands of Islamic imperialism, and who cries out that this aggression should now stop, makes the stalwarts of our secularism go mad with fury. They brand him as an enemy of public peace and national integration. They find in him a

Hindu fundamentalist, a Fascist, a Nazi, in fact, a fiend who is plotting a genocide of the "poor Muslim minority".

## DEMOCRATIC VERSUS FASCIST

This sixth pair of labels is not so much in fashion these days as it used to be at one time. The Leftists invoke these labels only when they are in search of a united front of all "democratic forces" in order to fight the "forces of fascism". They use the word "democratic" to entice some elements who do not rise immediately to the bait of a united front. And they hurl the word "fascist" when they find that their other swear-words like reactionary and revivalist etc., have failed to hurt.

The dictionaries define a democrat as "one who adheres to or promotes democracy as a principle", and a fascist as "one who believes in using forceful methods". These definitions make it quite easy to find out as to where the caps fit. The Leftists swear by democracy only so long as they are in the opposition. They believe and proclaim that they will use force to transform society once they are in power. They are convinced that they alone know what is good for the rest of the community. They divide every society into shepherds and sheep, reserving the former's role for themselves. Their self-righteousness and extreme intolerance of every other point of view mould them into first class fascists, whatever be the ism with which they adorn themselves. They promote and profit by an irrational and anti-intellectual atmosphere. They suspect and shout a conspiracy behind every move of every other party. It is, therefore, difficult to understand how the Leftists label themselves as democrats. But it is easy to understand why they denounce as fascists all those who do not subscribe to their aims and methods. It is simply a case of the thief crying thief.

## PROFITS OF PERVERSION

One cannot help concluding that the dictionaries are not at all helpful in deciphering the Leftist language. The source of that language has to be sought elsewhere. But one has also to notice that this language has so far proved very profitable for the Leftists. They have no roots in India, and are altogether an alien implant on our body-politic. But with the help of this language they have so far managed to pass as paragons of patriotism, progress, and public welfare.

One is reminded of a folk-tale from Haryana which illustrates the Leftist way of reasoning. A Jāt (peasant) was carrying a *khāt* (cot) on his head as he passed by the house of a Telī (oilman). The Telī was a poet. He burst out in rhyme: "*Jāt re Jāt, tere sir par khāt* (O you Jāt, on your head you have a *khāt*)." The Jāt was also a poet. He hit back: "*Telī re Telī tere sir par kolhū* (O you Teli, on your head you have a *kolhū*, an oilpress)." The Telī protested: "My friend, your lines do not rhyme." The Jāt smiled with self-satisfaction and said: "To hell with rhyme! Who cares for rhyme? What matters is that you are going to collapse under the weight of the *kolhū*."

That is exactly what is happening in India's politics. The so-called Rightists are collapsing under the weight of certain words which the Leftists have heaped upon their heads without rhyme or reason.

# 3

# The Source of the Leftist Language

Leftist professors and publicists claim that their language got formulated in the course of India's fight for freedom from British rule. They also claim that this language was used in order to characterise correctly the different forces and factions in the field at various stages of the struggle for freedom. This is a plain and a big lie. The annals of that freedom struggle provide no evidence that this language was used in India's politics till the late 'thirties of this century. Some prominent words of this language were totally absent from India's political parlance prior to that time. Some other words which we do find in that parlance were used to convey meanings that were entirely different from the meanings they acquired at a later stage. And even when these words became current in their present-day sense, their consumption was confined to a small Leftist coterie inside and outside the freedom movement. It was only after the attainment of independence that this parlance spread like a plague, particularly during the period when Pandit Jawaharlal Nehru and Indira Gandhi dominated the Indian political scene.

The record has, therefore, to be put straight. We have to go back to the actual political parlance which obtained in this country at different stages of the struggle for freedom. In the process, we shall discover not only the stage at which the Leftist language was interpolated into India's political parlance but also the source from which this language was imported or smuggled in.

### THE FIRST PHASE: THE LIBERAL LANGUAGE

India's fight for freedom started several decades before the Indian National Congress was founded in 1885. It assumed the form of a large-scale rebellion in North India in 1857. It was a mixed affair. In Delhi and Avadh, it was a *jihād* waged by Muslims with the aim of regaining political power. Elsewhere, Hindu chieftains and masses fought for freedom of the motherland. The rebellion failed and the repression that followed was brutal as well as widespread. But what is pertinent for our purpose at present is that throughout this period the British were talking about the white man's burden and the mission of

Christianity in the midst of a "primitive society". The Muslims under the leadership of Syed Ahmed Khan were crawling before the British, and seeking forgiveness. Hindus had fallen silent.

For almost two decades after 1857, national effort had perforce to be confined to religious revival, social reform, and cultural renaissance. The Indian National Congress, although founded by an Englishman, became a part of this broad national effort. The religious, social, and cultural movements were more powerful and pervasive. In fact, it was these non-political movements which shaped the political attitudes of different people who participated in Congress activities at different stages of the freedom movement.

The political parlance at this first stage consisted almost entirely of such phrases as had been made current by 19th century British liberalism. A majority of Englishmen and their press in this country did not look kindly at what they regarded as "the pretensions of natives and niggers". They started dubbing the Congress as a "Hindu organisation dominated by Bengali *bābūs*". Some Muslim politicians, who fancied themselves as scions of the erstwhile ruling race and successors to the Mughal Empire, picked up these British jibes. Their leader, Sir Syed Ahmed Khan, did some sabre-rattling on behalf of his community. The Congressites on their part tried to prove that the Congress was not a Hindu but a National organisation, thus making for the first time a distinction between "Hindu" and "National". They invited some prominent and willing Muslim gentlemen to preside over some annual sessions of the Congress, and paid the railway fare and other expenses of some Muslim delegates.

The only significant development at this stage was the juxtaposition of the word "Hindu" against the word "National". So far the two words had meant one and the same thing. This was the commencement of that political parlance which in, due course, reduced the national society to a mere "majority community" as against a colony crystallized by Islamic imperialism and now masquerading as the "Muslim minority". Both Hindu and Muslim politicians were sharing this parlance in common. But the word "communal" had not yet become an abusive political label. This word was used in its normal and neutral sense and that, too, when some one referred to the "communal question" for settling which some constitutional devices had to be sought for and found.

## THE SECOND STAGE: NATIONAL SELF-ASSERTION

The next stage arrived after the Partition of Bengal in 1905. The radical nationalist forces which had been maturing in the meanwhile leaped to the forefront. The old guard of the Congress felt the ground slipping from under is feet. It swam with the current to a certain distance. But basically it was not happy with this new turn of events. The showdown came at Surat in 1907. The old guard was able to save the situation for itself. However, the victory it won proved temporary as was to be seen very soon.

Some new words now appeared in the political parlance of India. The old guard started describing itself as "Moderates" while it denounced the other side as "Extremists". But the label which the new entrants used for themselves was "Nationalists", which camp included the revolutionaries dreaded by the old guard as well as the British rulers as "terrorists".

The Nationalists had to pass through the fire of British repression. But they survived the storm and captured the Congress after a few years. The Moderates had to withdraw from the national organisation to form their Liberal Federation. Meanwhile, the Nationalists had greatly impressed a new generation of Muslim politicians by the methods they used and the power they exercised over the mass mind. The Muslim politicians now started thinking loudly of joining hands with the Nationalists in order to settle their own parochial and pan-Islamic scores with the British.

It is a different story that the Nationalists led by Lokamanya Tilak failed to diagnose the motivations of Muslim politicians, and made several big concessions on issues of crucial importance when they signed the Congress-League Pact at Lucknow in 1916. So far as the political parlance of this period was concerned, the Nationalists were still known as Nationalists. Their opponents of earlier years, the Moderates, had sunk into oblivion, particularly after the advent of Mahatma Gandhi on the national scene. Nobody had as yet thought of calling the Nationalists by any other name. No word of the present-day political parlance had yet gained currency in the relevant writings and speeches of this period.

## THE THIRD STAGE: SOVIET SUBVERSION

The language of Nationalism, which had triumphed after a long struggle, was soon to be subverted by an alien and anti-national language. This new language had been coined by Lenin. It started stealing into India in the wake of the Bolshevik coup d'etat in Russia in November 1917. In subsequent years, the flow of finance from the Soviet Union became progressively more plentiful for the promotion of this language in India.

A Communist Party of India-a section of the Communist Internationale had been floated by M.N.Roy in far-off Tashkent in October 1920. Roy was a renegade from Nationalist ranks who had joined hands with Muslim *mujāhidīn*, and who was planning to arm and hurl the Pathans against the British rule. The plan failed and Roy retired to Moscow. The national movement would not have noticed the Party for quite some time but for several conspiracy cases which the British Government of India launched against it with great fanfare between 1924 and 1929. The language which the hirelings of Moscow spoke in the courts attracted the attention of Nationalist revolutionaries. Most of them were men of action rather than men of thought. Their battle-cry so for had been *Vande Mātaram*. Now they took to shouting *Inqilāb Zindābād* also.

Later on, the British Government made another major contribution to the spread of the language coined in the Soviet slave empire. It imposed a ban on the Communist Party and proscribed the circulation of Communist literature, thus bestowing an aura of martyrdom and mystery on both. On the other hand, it made the same Communist literature easily available to Nationalist revolutionaries rotting in its jails in order to wean them away from the path of what it described as "terrorism". Many of these sterling patriots became convinced Communists while they were still in prison. When they came out, they swelled the ranks of the Communist Party, and started serving the interests of Soviet imperialism. But in the eyes of the public at large, they still retained the stature which they had earned earlier in the service of the motherland.

## CONVEYOR-BELTS OF COMMUNIST LANGUAGE

But, in spite of all these favourable factors, Communist language would have remained confined to party cadres had it not been espoused and popularised by an important leader inside the national movement. That was Pandit Jawaharlal Nehru. He had been recruited in the international Communist network by M.N.Roy, and taken to Europe in 1926 for being brainwashed by participation in the meetings of various

Communist fronts. And he started using Communist language when he presided over a momentous session of the Indian National Congress in 1929-30. Because of his westernised upbringing and education, he had always felt ill-at-ease with the language of Nationalism which had its source in India's own history and cultural heritage. He was also dissatisfied with the language of 19th century liberalism which he had so far shared with the British. The Communist language, therefore, came to him as a great relief. He lapped it up immediately and digested it in large doses.*

Pandit Nehru also would have ploughed a lonely furrow in the national movement if Communist thought and language had not in the meanwhile spread to all prestigious seats of learning in the West. We are not going into the reasons of this spread-out. Suffice it to say that, in many respects, Communism was only a continuation of Capitalist thought-processes with which the West had been familiar for a long time. What is relevant for our purpose at present is that many Indians who went to Western universities in the late 'twenties and early 'thirties imbibed Communist thought and came back talking Communist language. Particularly, the London School of Economics under Harold Laski poisoned a whole generation of Indian students. Some of them became professors in Indian universities, and passed on the lore to their students. Some others became journalists and politicians who processed Indian politics in terms of Communist categories of thought, and made Communist language popular among an increasing number of politically conscious people. All this had a multiplier effect. And by the middle of the 'thirties, Pandit Nehru had a solid bastion of support inside as well outside the national movement, particularly among the English-educated intelligentsia.

So when Pandit Nehru became Congress president for the second time in 1936, the whole political atmosphere had become chock-full of Communist catch-phrases — bourgeois and proletarian, class struggle and class collaboration, revolution and reaction, bourgeois nationalism and proletarian internationalism, bourgeois democracy and proletarian dictatorship, progressive role and reactionary resistance, fascist forces and the democratic front, etc. Many a periodical and pamphlet published in English and other Indian languages was spreading the Com-

*See Sita Ram Goel, *The Genesis and Growth* of *Nehruism,* Volume I, *Commitment to Communism,* Voice of India, 1993

munist jargon at an accelerated speed.

This was a highly technical, almost an esoteric, language. Lenin had used common parlance words to convey his own Communist meanings and messages. No one who was not conversant with the Leninist lore could decipher this language with the help of ordinary dictionaries. Small wonder, therefore, that the Nationalists led by Mahatma Gandhi failed to understand the nature, purpose, and role of this language, though they suspected it as something insidious. Some Nationalists picked up parts of this language in order to sound in tune with the times. Some others were thrown on the defensive when they were lambasted by this language. A Socialist Party had crystallized within the Indian National Congress. Its members spoke the Communist language with great gusto although unlike the Communist Party cadre they were not hirelings of the Soviet Union.

## COMMUNISTS IDENTIFIED BUT NOT COMMUNIST LANGUAGE

The Communists were found out as a Soviet fifth-column by the Socialists in 1939-40, and by the Indian National Congress as a whole during 1942-45. They were expelled form the national organisation in 1945. But Communist thought and language were neither re-examined nor purged simultaneously or in subsequent years. The dominance of Pandit Nehru for 17 years in the post-independence period widened the field for Communist language. It spread like a forest fire. His daughter, Indira Gandhi handed over to a Communist clique the commanding positions in the Indian National Congress and the country at large. The only difference between the father and the daughter was that while the patriarch was a sincere fellow-traveller, the daughter played the game purely for purposes of demagogy aimed at consolidating personal power.

Several political parties have been formed by factions which have walked out of the Congress. But these splits have taken place solely on the basis of personalities, and seldom for the sake of ideology. The new parties have severed their links with the Congress organisation but not with what is known as "Congress culture". And this culture consists almost entirely of the same catch-phrases which were popularised by Pandit Nehru.

There has been only one political party — the Jana Sangh turned BJP — which has grown outside the Congress, and which started with an ideology and language of its own. But over the years, this party also has tended to shed its ideological identity. It has picked up progressively India's prevailing political parlance. This parlance is supposed to be the only gateway to popular vote and political power which, we are told privately by this party, will be used for nationalist purposes. The road to hell is often paved with good intentions. In any case, in India at present we have a multiplicity of parties but a unity of slogans.

## THE COMMUNIST LANGUAGE IS A LANGUAGE OF IMPERIALISM

There is thus no truth whatsoever in the Leftist claim that India's prevailing political parlance took shape in the course of India's fight for freedom against British imperialism. On the contrary, this parlance was imported from the Soviet Union by a Soviet fifth-column and with the help of Soviet finances. And it became predominant only towards the fag end of the freedom struggle.

A close scrutiny of the Communist language shows that it has an affinity with the languages used earlier by Islamic, Christian, and British imperialism. That should surprise no one. The language of imperialism is the same in all ages and everywhere. India has been able to save herself from total subversion so far only because the spirit of Indian Nationalism has surfaced again and again. But that spirit is not inexhaustible and will not serve indefinitely unless Indian Nationalism evolves and starts speaking a language of its own.

# 4

# The Character of Leftist Language

Ever since its inauguration in the opening years of this century, the language of Leftism has been the loudest in denouncing this or that imperialism. Quite often, it has imagined or invented an imperialism where none existed. This exercise has helped it to hide the fact that it itself is the latest language of imperialism.

Imperialism down the ages has evolved and employed a number of languages. The verbiage has varied according to differences of time and clime. But all languages of imperialism have shared certain characteristics in common. The language of Leftism passes this test quite creditably.

## CHARACTERISTICS OF AN IMPERIALIST LANGUAGE

To start with, every language of imperialism invokes an inscrutable entity as its source and sanction. This entity reveals its final and irreversible will to a unique person. All pronouncements of this person are placed beyond the reach of human reason and experience. They have to be accepted on faith. Compared to faith, reason and experience are found to be faulty faculties. These faculties can fulfil themselves only if they follow and fortify faith.

Second, every language of imperialism divides human history into two sharply separated periods — an age of darkness which prevailed before the mission of the unique person is announced, and an age of light which follows thereafter. The entire past history of every nation preceding the age of light is painted black so that nothing in which a nation can take pride is left unscathed.

Third, every language of imperialism divides the human family into two mutually exclusive camps — the believers who accept the dogmas propounded by the unique person, and the unbelievers who doubt or reject those dogmas. The believers are placed under a categorical imperative to make war on the unbelievers till the latter are either converted or killed off. The believers do not have to be better human beings in terms of moral character or mental competence. It is sufficient if they have fervour and ferocity born of faith.

Fourth, every language of imperialism bands together all believers everywhere into a brotherhood which cuts across all national bounds of geography, history, and culture. Every nation is invited to renounce its independent identity and become a colony of the country where the unique person was born, or where his dogmas first acquired the backing of brute armed force. This dead uniformity into which all nations are to be steam-rollered is hailed as universality.

Fifth, every language of imperialism propounds that the inscrutable entity has mandated the whole earth to the brotherhood of the believers. So when the brotherhood or any section of it mounts an aggression, it automatically becomes a war of liberation. The brotherhood is only claiming what already belongs to it. The native people who have lived in a land for ages past lose all their rights, and become mere squatters in their own homeland which no longer belongs to them.

Sixth, every language of imperialism lays down two inevitabilities — an inevitable victory of the believers, and an inevitable defeat of the unbelievers. The believers are told that the inscrutable entity is on their side, and that no power on earth can stop their onward march. The believers are thus enthused so that they spare no effort, and the unbelievers are demoralised so that they surrender or offer only half-hearted resistance.

Seventh, every language of imperialism equips the believers with an immeasurable degree of self-righteousness. They are told that the lives, liberties, properties, and honour of the unbelievers have already been forfeited in their favour by the inscrutable entity. They are also told that they commit no crime when they kill, and enslave, and plunder, and humiliate the unbelievers. This gives a good conscience to the believers for indulging in an endless spree of bloodshed and vandalism. In fact, their crimes become meritorious deeds.

Lastly, the unbelievers are accused of all sorts of crimes which they are supposed to have committed by the very fact of their being what they are. In fact, the whole life-history of every unbeliever becomes a catalogue of crimes. The unbelievers are thus debarred from any sympathy from any quarters. At the same time, the crimes committed against them are explained away in term of their supposed crimes.

In the lines that follow, I will present a panoramic view of those languages of imperialism which have invaded India, at one time or the other. Incidentally, the list is exhaustive because India has been plagued by every principal language of imperialism invented by human ingenuity so far.

## THE LANGUAGE OF ISLAMIC IMPERIALISM

The language of Islamic imperialism was the first language of imperialism to invade India. Its standard-bearers were the Arab and the Turkish armies which came in successive waves from the middle of the 7th to the middle of the 18th century. It had proclaimed :

1. Allah had revealed his final and irreversible will to Muhammad bin Abdullah who was born in Mecca in AD 570 and who proclaimed himself as the Last Prophet in AD 610;
2. Human history before Muhammad proclaimed his prophethood was *jāhiliyyah* (era of ignorance), and the light of truth dawned on earth only after that date;
3. That date divided mankind into *mu'mins* (believers) and *kāfirs* (unbelievers), and the *mu'mins* should become *mujāhids* (holy warriors) by waging *jihād* (holy war) against the *kāfirs;*
4. All *mu'mins* everywhere were members of the *ummah* (brotherhood) which recognised no national frontiers or peculiarities of national culture;
5. Allah had mandated the entire earth, including Sind and Hind, to the *ummah* which had thus acquired an inalienable right to conquer Sind and Hind and cleanse them of *kufr* (infidelism);
6. The triumph of the *ummah* was inevitable in Sind and Hind, as elsewhere, and the *mujāhids* should make all efforts to expedite that end;
7. Allah who was *al-Rahmān al-Rahīm* (the Compassionate, the Merciful) had already forfeited the lives, liberties, properties, and honour of Hindu *kāfirs,* and the *mujāhids* should kill the Hindus, capture their women and children, plunder their properties, demolish their temples, desecrate their idols, burn their scriptures, humiliate their holy men, and extirpate every vestige of their culture;
8. Hindus were wallowing in the sin of *kufr and shirk* (idolatry) and fully deserved the punishment meted out to them by the *mu'mins.*

This is not the place to tell the story of Islamic imperialism in India — how Hindus refused to be impressed by Allah and his gibberish (the Quran and the Sunnah), and how they waged a long-drawn-out war of resistance till the barbarians were brought to book. What is relevant in the present context is that although Hindus overcame Islamic imperialism, they failed to see through the language of that imperialism. Hindu masses continued to react with revulsion towards everything Islamic. But Hindu saints, scholars, scribes, social reformers, and politicians came to accept Islam as a religion as good as their own Sanātana Dharma. This self-deception is still working as a potent poison in whatever remains of India after more than thirteen hundred years of Islamic aggression.

## THE LANGUAGE OF CHRISTIAN IMPERIALISM

The next language of imperialism to plague India was that of Christian imperialism. It first came to this country in the company of Portuguese pirates in the opening years of the 16th century. Some of these pirates such as Francis Xavier were dressed as priests and friars and introduced themselves as soldiers of Jesus Christ. It was this latter tribe which trumpeted:

1. The Only True God had sent his Only-begotten Son, Christ Jesus, to atone for the sins of all mankind by dying on the Cross in Jerusalem in AD 33;
2. Human history before the Crucifixion of Jesus was an era of darkness, and the light of divinity descended on earth exactly on that date;
3. Mankind became divided into Christians and heathens after the advent of Jesus, and the Christians were under a divine obligation to wage an unceasing crusade against the heathens;
4. All Christians everywhere were united in the Catholic Church, the Body as well the Bride of Jesus and the Holy Mother of Mankind, which recognised no national divisions or distinctions;
5. The Only True God had mandated the entire earth including India to the Catholic Church which had thus inherited an inalienable right to liberate India, as all other lands, from the horrors of heathenism;
6. The victory of the Catholic Church over India, as elsewhere, was inevitable, and soldiers of Christ Jesus should endeavour to expedite that end;
7. The Only True God, in his infinite mercy, had forfeited the lives, liberties, properties, and honour of the Gentoo (Hindu) heathens, and the Catholic Church was authorised to demolish their temples, to smash their idols, to burn their scriptures, to perse-

cute their priests, to close down their schools, to prohibit their public celebrations, to sequester their movable and immovable possessions, to separate them from their children, to convert their women into concubines for the soldiers of Christ Jesus, to exile those sections of their population which proved recalcitrant, and to massacre those who offered armed resistance;

8. The Gentoo heathens had lived for long in the sin and shame of polytheism and pantheism and fornication with false gods, and their crimes deserved drastic punishment.

This is not the place to narrate why conversions to Christianity remained confined to some small sections of Hindu society, and how the bulk of that society repudiated the falsehoods retailed by the Christian missionaries. What is relevant in the present context is that in spite of the crimes committed by Christianity in India, a section of the English-educated Hindu elite became enamoured of this creed and recognised it as a religion. That mistake has enabled Christian imperialism to continue staking its claims and making inroads into Hindu society.

## THE LANGUAGE OF WESTERN (BRITISH) IMPERIALISM

The language of Western imperialism came to India as the language of British imperialism. But it was shared in common by the French, the Dutch, the Portuguese, the Belgians, the Italians, the Germans, and the Russians who had enslaved many nations in Asia and Africa by force of superior arms. For all practical purposes, it was the old language of Christian imperialism. But it was dressed up in a secular verbiage. Its tenets were as follows:

1. The march of human history had proved the cultural superiority of the white man, and placed him in the vanguard of human progress;
2. Human history before the 16th century was an age of barbarism, and an era of enlightenment had commenced since then;
3. Mankind was now divided into the civilised people of Europe on the one hand, and the savage races of Asia, Africa, and America on the other;
4. The white race was a distinct fraternity designated by history to dominate the whole world, including India;
5. History had placed the people of India in charge of the white men from Britain who should bear the burden of their civilising

mission without bothering about the negative attitude of the natives;

6. History was heading towards an inevitable triumph of the Western civilisation, and the British should work towards that fulfilment in India as in many other lands conquered by them;
7. History had rendered out of date the political system, social order, economic organisation, and cultural traditions of India, and the British should smash them by force or reform them out of recognition, without any hesitation;.
8. Hindus had lived for long in a medley of primitive superstitions and amply deserved whatever suffering the British civilising mission had imposed upon them.

This is not the place to tell how the British proceeded with their civilising mission in this country, and what havoc they wrought in course of a hundred and fifty years. What is relevant in the present context is that although the British Raj has departed, the language of British imperialism has survived almost intact in the language of our brown sahibs who have inherited the British mantle. India to them is a backward or underdeveloped or developing country which should look to the West, particularly the United States of America, for ideological inspiration as well as concrete models in all matters of major and minor importance. This has reduced the Indian elite to brown apes of the West, and the Indian people to a pack of handicapped children. The havoc which the language of British imperialism is still continuing to work in all spheres of Indian life belies description.

### THE LANGUAGE OF COMMUNIST IMPERIALISM

The language of Communist imperialism started trickling into India soon after the Bolsheviks seized power in Russia in November 1917. Leading Western thinkers like Bertrand Russell have identified Communism as a Christian heresy. Small wonder that the language of Communist imperialism is the same as that of Christian imperialism, except for the Marxist trappings in which Lenin has disguised it. This becomes obvious when we contemplate its following features:

1. Forces of Production, maturing in the womb of History, found a matchless midwife in comrade Lenin in, and a field for their fullest free play in Soviet Russia after the Revolution in 1917;
2. History, which had so far been a history of class oppression and class struggle, now took a decisive turn towards a classless society;
3. The whole world, including India, now became a battle-ground

between forces of feudal and capitalist reaction on the one hand, and forces of proletarian revolution on the other;

4. The proletariat in every country, including India, became part of an internationale comraderie which had no use for nationalism in any shape or form;
5. History had mandated the whole earth, including India, to the Communist Internationale, the vanguard of the world proletariat, and it was the inalienable right Internationale to promote a proletarian revolution in every country;
6. The victory of the Internationale was inevitable, and its sections in different countries should endeavour to expedite that end;
7. History had pronounced as outmoded all existing political, social, cultural and economic institutions in India, and the Communist Party of India, a section of the Communist Internationale, should smash them so that the last vestiges of feudalism, capitalism and colonialism were wiped out;
8. The feudal lords and capitalists in India had conspired with British imperialism in order to keep the Indian people enslaved, and they deserved to be destroyed together with their political conspiracy, the Indian National Congress.

This is not the place to tell how the Communist Party of India has functioned as a fifth-column of Soviet Russia for nearly sixty-seven* years. What is relevant in the present context is that, although the Communist Party of India has failed to consolidate any substantial political base beyond West Bengal and Kerala, the spread of the language of Communist imperialism has been phenomenal due to causes which we have described in a previous chapter. By now, this language has become the standard language of Secularism in India, whatever be the names by which various political parties and factions describe themselves.

What is still more significant, the language of Communist imperialism operates in close cooperation with the languages of Islamic, Christian, and Western imperialism and has succeeded, for the time being, in silencing or putting on the defensive whatever is still left of the language of Indian Nationalism. This becomes crystal clear when we examine the history and role of the Leftist language ever since it invaded India in the early 'twenties of this century.

* This was written in 1984. Since then the Soviet Union has collapsed.

# 5

# The History of Leftist Language

The first major spokesman of the Leftist language for India was M.N.Roy in his *India in Transition* which was published from Paris in 1922. He formulated in this book practically all the slogans which have been the stock-in-trade of Leftists ever since. Of course, he was not the invèntor of the lore. He had learnt it from Lenin.

It will facilitate an understanding of Roy's formulations if we survey briefly the background of Indian Nationalism as it had developed prior to that period. There are certain key words and phrases used by Roy which may cause confusion unless they are clarified in advance.

## TWO SCHOOLS OF INDIAN NATIONALISM

The freedom movement against British imperialism since the Revolt of 1857 had witnessed a debate between two schools of thought. On the one hand, there were those who regarded the British rule in India as a divine dispensation, and who aspired to remould India in the image of 19th century Britain, particularly in the matter of political institutions. They dominated the Indian National Congress till the Swadeshi Movement (1905-1910) swept them away. Roy refers to them as bourgeois liberals, modern intellectuals, radical leaders, moderates, radical intelligentsia and also as 'denationalised' intellectuals, which name had been bestowed upon them by the opposite school of nationalist thought. On the other hand, there were those who regarded the British rule as an evil imposed upon India by force of arms, and who wanted to build a free India on the basis of values and visions enshrined in India's ancient spirituality and culture. They came to the fore in the Indian National Congress during the Swadeshi Movement, and took command of the freedom struggle under the leadership of Mahatma Gandhi. Roy refers to them as orthodox nationalists, radical nationalists, extremists, and Hindu nationalists. He makes a distinction between Hindu Nationalism and Indian Nationalism which, according to him, was a more comprehensive term.

## FUNDAMENTAL FORMULATIONS OF ROY

M.N. Roy had been sent abroad by the Bengal revolutionaries in

1915 in search of German arms. The Germans did not live upto the promises they had made, and Roy wandered away through China and Japan into the USA where he was positively impressed by the modern Western civilisation. Next, he went to Mexico where he came in contact with Communist thought. That cured him completely of whatever love was still left in him for India's ancient culture. Finally, he landed in the Soviet Union in 1920, and became a confidant of Lenin. He functioned as a leading luminary of the Communist Internationale for several years.

But Roy's ardour for an armed revolution in India had not cooled. He tried to take a trainload of Russian arms to the Pathans on India's north-west frontier. A number of *muhājirin*[1] joined him with great enthusiasm. They had left India during the Khilafat agitation, and were looking for foreign arms in order to re-establish a *Dār al Islām* in this country. The plan failed because Amir Habibullah of Afghanistan, who had promised a passage, was bought over by the British, and blocked the path of this Communist-cum-Islamic brigade. A few years later, Roy had to flee from the Soviet Union where serious charges had been levelled against him, including embezzlement of huge funds meant for financing a Communist revolution in India. He was recruited by the British Intelligence, brought to India under the cover of a revolutionary avoiding arrest, put in jail for a few years, and hoisted up as a martyr. He was meant to serve as an ideological bullet aimed mainly at Mahatma Gandhi. Ever since, the only hardware that remained in his hands was his pen which he plied with great prowess.

Roy pronounced as follows on India's history, culture, people and politics:

1. India had never been a nation before the British conquest. "At the time of the British conquest, that is, towards the middle of the 18th century, the economic and political evolution of India was such that her people could be called *rather a number of nationalities inhabiting a continent than a composite national unit*" (G. Adhikari (ed.), *Documents of the History of the Communist Party of India*, New Delhi, 1971, p. 382, Italics added).
2. The Revolt of 1857 was a reactionary flare-up of decadent feu-

1. Indian Muslims who had migrated to Afghanistan during the Khilafat Movement (1920-22) in keeping with the Prophet's directive that Muslims living in countries ruled by non-Muslims should either wage *jihād* against the infidel government, or migrate to Muslim countries.

dalism. "Socially it was a reactionary movement because it wanted to replace British rule by revived feudal imperialism, either of the Moghuls or of the Marathas" (ibid., p. 383).

3. Indian people by themselves were incapable of evolving political consciousness, or patriotism, or nationalism. "The overwhelming majority of the population lived in villages, steeped in ignorance and submerged in social stagnation. Politics, forms of government, national subjugation or freedom remained outside their concern and beyond their comprehension" (ibid., p. 383).
4. The Western-oriented Indian intellectuals alone were pioneers of progress. "The only section of the people showing any sign of life was the modern intellectuals educated in Western methods and thoughts. These 'denationalised' intellectuals were instrumental in bringing to India, *for the first time in her long eventful history,* political patriotism" (ibid., pp. 383–84, Italics added).
5. Evolutionary nationalism led by the Western-oriented intellectuals, was a revolutionary movement. "The constitutional democracy or the evolutionary nationalism advocated by liberal bourgeoisie led by the intellectuals spelled doom to the old social heritage and religious orthodoxy. And these *revolutionary forces* were crystallizing in the Congress under radical leaders whose programme was not to revive the India of the rishis with its contented handicraft workers saturated with ignorance and dosed in the name of religion, but to build a new society on the ruins of the old" (ibid., pp. 389–90, Italics added).
6. The British Government was the best government which India had ever had in her long history. "The struggle of the radical intelligentsia was not against an effete and antiquated political institution but for the democratisation of the existing government which... was the most advanced that the country had till then" (ibid., p. 384).
7. Orthodox nationalism advocated by the other school of Congressites was a reactionary movement. "Orthodox nationalism, in the social sense, was the resistance of forces of reaction against the ominous radicalism of the 'denationalised' intellectuals who led the Congress. The same forces whose military explosion was the Mutiny of 1857, could be discovered behind the political theories of the orthodox nationalism of half a century later" (ibid., p. 390,).

8. Hindu nationalism of Swami Vivekananda was spiritual imperialism. "Although its political philosopher and leader were found subsequently in the persons of Aurobindo Ghose and Bipin Chandra Pal, respectively, its fundamental ideology was conceived by a young intellectual of petit-bourgeois origin. He was Narendra Nath Dutt, subsequently known by the religious nomenclature of Swami Vivekananda... Like Tilak, Dutt was also a prophet of Hindu nationalism. He was also a believer in the cultural superiority of the Indian people, and held that on this cultural basis should be built the future Indian nation... He preached that Hinduism, not Indian nationalism, should be aggressive. His nationalism was a spiritual imperialism" (ibid., pp. 391–92).
9. The revolutionaries inspired by Swami Vivekananda and the Swadeshi Movement were victims of reaction. "Thus an intelligently rebellious element which otherwise would have been the vanguard of the exploited class in a social struggle, had to give in to national pre-occupations and contribute itself to a movement for the immediate overthrow of foreign rule, not for progress forward, but in order to go back to an imaginary golden age, the fountain-head of India's spiritual heritage... In their religiousness and wild spiritual imperialism, they embodied the reactionary social forces" (ibid., p. 393).
10. The non-cooperation movement led by Mahatma Gandhi was exploitation of the ignorance of the Indian masses. "The extremists, now called non-cooperators, have had better success than moderates in drawing the masses under the influence of nationalism... But they could not develop the potentiality of the mass movement by leading it in accordance with its economic urges and social tendencies. Their tactics was to strengthen the nationalist movement by the questionable method of exploiting the ignorance of the masses. And the best way of exploiting the ignorance of the masses was to make a religion of nationalism. This tactics led to the appearance of Mohan Das Karamchand Gandhi on the political horizon, and the eclipse of all other politico-social tendencies in the shade of Gandhism" (ibid., p. 394).
11. Gandhism was the most reactionary form of Indian nationalism. "In Gandhism culminate all the social tendencies that have always differentiated the principal tendencies of Indian nationalism. *In fact, Gandhism is the acutest and most desperate mani-*

*festation of the forces of reaction trying to hold their own against the objectively revolutionary tendencies contained in the liberal bourgeois nationalism.* The impending wane of Gandhism signifies the collapse of the reactionary forces and their total elimination from the political movement" (ibid., pp. 394–95, Italics added).

12. Finally, Mahatma Gandhi was speaking essentially the same language as was spoken earlier by Lokmanya Tilak, Sri Aurobindo and Bipin Chandra Pal. "Although somewhat unique in its idiosyncrasies and fanaticism, the Gandhi cult is not an innovation. Divested of the rebellious spirit and the shrewd politician in him, *Tilak would resemble Gandhi in so far as religious belief and spiritual prejudices are concerned.* But for his versatility in modern thought and characteristic looseness of conviction, *Bipin Chandra Pal would perchance join the Mahatma in the passionate denunciation of everything that adds to the material comfort of man.* Had he been more of a monomaniac than a profound thinker with metaphysical preoccupations, *Aurobindo Ghose would subscribe to Gandhi's philosophy*" (ibid., pp. 396–97, Italics added).

## CONTINUED CANNONADE

Gandhism did not wane, nor did the "reactionary forces" collapse immediately as anticipated by Roy in 1922. They continued to dominate the Indian political scene for another two decades and more. On the other hand, Roy was expelled from the Communist Internationale in 1929 for a number of "counter-revolutionary crimes". But Roy's formulations and language became the bedrock of Leftist stance and slogans for all time to come. This happened because these formulations were not a product of any original thinking on the part of Roy. His own mind was too poor for any worthwhile ideological performance. He was only repeating, parrot-like, the standard language of Communist imperialism as he had learnt it from Lenin.

M.N. Roy's place as the mentor of the Communist Party of India was taken over by R. Palme-Dutt of the Communist Party of Great Britain. He had already fired his first fusillade against Mahatma Gandhi in his *Modern India* published from London in 1926. "Gandhi failed," wrote Palme-Dutt, "as the leader of the national struggle because he could not cut himself loose from the upper class interests and prejudices in which he had been brought up...The 'spirituality' of Gandhi is only the expression of this class interest. All parasitic and propertied classes have to weave around themselves a fog of confused language, superstition, tradition, religion, revivalism etc., in order to hide from the masses the fact of their exploitation" (p.72). Once again, a mindless minion was relaying his master's voice from Moscow.

Two years later, the Sixth Congress of the Communist Internationale declared a veritable war on Gandhism. In an enumeration of "ideologies among the working class inimical to Communism", it proclaimed, "Tendencies like Gandhism in India, thoroughly imbued with religious conception, idolize the most backward and economically reactionary forms of social life, see the solution of social problems not in proletarian socialism but in a reversion to these backward forms, preach passivity and repudiate class struggle, and in the process of the development of the revolution become transformed into an openly reactionary force. Gandhism is more and more becoming an ideology directed against mass revolution. It must be strongly combated by Communism."

The Communist hysteria against Mahatma Gandhi went on mounting till Palme-Dutt wrote in 1931 that "To all that is young and generous in India the name of Gandhi is an object of cursing and contempt, the name of Judas".[2]

## PERCOLATION OF THE POISON

The language of Communist imperialism was borrowed, lock, stock and barrel, by the Congress Socialist Party which was formed inside the Indian National Congress in 1934 under inspiration from Pandit Nehru who was the tallest among the native converts. Unlike the Communists, the Socialists had no organisational or financial links with the Communist Internationale which had by now become a helpless instrument of Soviet foreign policy. But they agreed with the Communists in their evaluation of Indian history, society, culture, and current politics. The only point on which the two differed was the personality and role of Mahatma Gandhi. The Communists regarded him as the "cleverest bourgeois scoundrel". The Socialists, on the other hand, had admiration for his qualities of head and heart, and were convinced that he alone could mobilise the masses though they were

2. *Labour Monthly*, London, May 1931, p. 264

not at all happy about "Gandhiji ganging up with the Birlas instead of leading the workers and peasants for national liberation and social revolution".

The Socialists have travelled far, and in a different direction, since those days of dalliance with Communism. But their disenchantment is confined only to forms of polity and society. They have never been able to cure themselves of their love for the Leftist language in the context of Indian nationalism. They continue to pass on to us such Leftist terms as communalist, chauvinist, fascist, revivalist, and reactionary intended for all those who regard Hindu society as the core and mainstay of the Indian nation. All this has landed them in a love-hate relationship with the Communists. They feel irresistibly drawn whenever the Communists dangle before them the bait of a united front against Hindu Communalism and social reaction. But they feel uncomfortable when the Communists reveal their true character as servitors of the Soviet Union.[3]

Meanwhile, the Communist Party of India itself has split into several factions. The struggle between Stalin and Trotsky which ended with the latter's defeat, had led some small groups to part company with the Communist Party. The scars, however, were too small to show. It was the breach between the Soviet Union and Red China in the 'sixties which really splintered the Communist Party into several factions.

On the other hand, some groups which left the Indian National Congress at different times and for different reasons, have moved closer to the Communists. The Forward Bloc founded by Netaji Subhash Chandra Bose was the earliest to do so after years of bitter feud with its future friends. In later years, Sanjay Gandhi's supremacy in the Congress not only stopped Communist infiltration and take-over of the Congress but also forced some fellow-travellers out of it. Today, these "exiles" sing the same songs as the Communists.[4]

Taken together, the Leftists in India constitute a far-flung phalanx which may not be solid within but which presents a united front without. It is easy to spot them because they adorn themselves with labels like communist, democratic, Leninist, Marxist, radical, revolutionary, socialist etc., in different permutations and combinations. There is little

3. That dilemma has disappeared with the disappearance of the Soviet Union. Now the Socialists and the Communists are comrades in arms.

4. The story has been repeated recently when V.P. Singh and company left the Congress. They walked straight into the Leftist parlour.

hope that they can ever come to power without direct intervention by the Soviet Union.[5] But their potential for purveying the poison of Leftist language is considerable. Indian Nationalism, which remains their topmost target, has to guard against them.

5. That hope has now been dashed with the disappearance of the Soviet Union.

# 6

# The Role of Leftist Language

The language of Communist imperialism continued to lambast the Congress leadership, particularly Mahatma Gandhi, for the latter's "failure to mobilize the toiling masses towards an immediate overthrow of the British rule in India". But when the Congress launched a mass movement in March 1930, the spokesmen of this language kept strictly aloof from it. Instead, they published a *Draft Plan of Action* in December 1930, characterising the Congress as a "class organisation of the capitalists working against the fundamental interests of the toiling masses". And they tried to sabotage the freedom struggle by splitting the trade union movement over which they had acquired some hold with the help of substantial finances flowing from the Soviet Union.

The song changed suddenly in 1935. The Soviet Union was feeling threatened by the rapid militarisation and rising anti-Communist tone of Nazi Germany. She was now seriously in search of mutual security pacts with Britain and France. But the governments in London and Paris had refused to respond to Soviet diplomatic feelers. The Communist Internationale, therefore, sent out a call to the Communist parties of Britain and France to strive for a "broad national front of all anti-fascist forces". The purpose was to build pressures for such Popular Front governments in London and Paris as would be amenable to Soviet approaches.

The Communist Party of France was strong. It had an ally also in a strong Socialist Party at home. So it succeeded on its own in securing a Popular Front government in Paris. But the Communist Party of Great Britain was too weak to exert any pressure on a strong conservative government in London. That task was, therefore, assigned to the Communist parties in the British colonies. The biggest and the most powerful of these parties was the Communist Party of India. This party was instructed to join the Indian National Congress via the newly formed Congress Socialist Party, and to push the national organisation towards another mass movement.

That was how the Congress Socialists ceased to be "petit-bourgeois Left-reformists" and became "the revolutionary Left-wing of the Indian National Congress". The Congress itself ceased to be a "class organisation of the Indian landlords and capitalists" and became a "broad national front of all patriotic people". The language of Communist imperialism was employing no end of casuistry to prove that a "Popular Front government in London was the best guarantee for an early dawn of freedom and democracy in India". The Congress Socialists Party was a worshipper of the Soviet Union as a proletarian paradise. It swallowed this language, hook, line and sinker. Pandit Jawaharlal Nehru who had by now become the draftsman of Congress resolutions, particularly on foreign policy, packed them with Communist phrases and swear-words. The language of Communist imperialism was fast getting transformed into the language of Leftism.

## SPLIT IN THE NATIONAL MOVEMENT

The Congress leadership under Mahatma Gandhi had, in the meanwhile, moved in an opposite direction. It was toying with the idea of trying the experiment in provincial self-government envisaged in the Government of India Act, 1935. The Leftists led by Pandit Nehru immediately launched a campaign against the "Rightist leadership" which was "trying to compromise with British imperialism in the interests of feudal and capitalist elements and against the interests of the toiling masses". At the same time they claimed that the "Left wing of the Congress was working for a democratisation of the national organisation by bringing into its fold the peasantry and the working class so that this organisation could play a revolutionary role at home and an anti-fascist role in international affairs".

As we have pointed out, the chief patron of this Leftist language inside the Congress was Pandit Nehru. Formally, he kept aloof from the Communist-Socialist combine. But he used it surreptitiously in order to hurl all sorts of insinuations, innuendos, and invectives on Sardar Patel whom he considered to be his main opponent in the Congress High Command. The Sardar had a healthy contempt for the Leftists and their language. But he was a man of few words who deemed it below his dignity to descend to the level of Leftism. The Leftist campaign, therefore, succeeded to a large extent in pillorying the Sardar as an "arch reactionary in alliance with the Birlas", and as a "fascist out to suppress all democratic, progressive, revolutionary, and socialist elements in the Congress". Quite a few other members of the High Command who were supporters of the Sardar, got tarred with the same brush.

The Congress had thrown up several contending schools of thought in the course of its development, and it was not unoften that issues had been debated on its platform with considerable heat. But all its debates so far had been homegrown, and related to India's problems. It was now for the first time that the Congress stood split by slogans imported from abroad and in the interests of a foreign power which had its own scores to settle in the power politics of Europe. The issues on which the Leftists were generating heat had little relevance to the Indian situation.

Finally, the Leftists were able to egg on Subhash Chandra Bose to challenge the leadership of Mahatma Gandhi, only to leave him in the lurch at the last moment when wires were pulled from Moscow. A number of sterling patriots had to leave the Congress to form the Forward Bloc. In due course, the Leftist pressure inside the Congress became strong enough to force a premature resignation by Congress ministries, soon after the Second World War broke out. The field was thus left clear for the Muslim League to spread its tentacles and mount its campaign for Pakistan.

## STANDARDS OF PUBLIC LIFE LOWERED

The so-called Congress Right had many people in its ranks who had renounced inherited wealth or self-earned fortunes or lucrative professions, and who had chosen to lead a life of poverty in the service of the motherland. Who could match Sardar Patel when it came to making sacrifice for the national cause? But these people became branded as reactionaries and fascists simply because they refused to serve the Soviet Union. On the other hand, the so-called Congress Left had quite a few people who were living in luxury on incomes derived from landed estates or from shares held in capitalist companies. But they were now strutting around as democrats, progressives, revolutionaries and socialists merely by mouthing certain slogans. They were making the best of both the worlds—living lavishly while proclaiming their love for the poor. Pandit Jawaharlal Nehru was a typical example.

The most significant contribution made to India's politics and public life by the language of Leftism was character assassination. Most of the time, the Leftists were poor in facts and logic but prolific in foul language. It opened the floodgates for all sorts of questionable characters to come forward and occupy the front seats on the public stage. The full harvest of the seeds sown in the years before independence was reaped in the post-independence period when politics and public life became progressively a safe haven for all sorts of scoundrels masquerading as servants of the people.

And it was not only the dichotomy between personal and public life which got deepened. The rational in man suffered a still more serious blow. Differences of opinion could no more be settled by reference to recorded facts or to logic or to the universe of discourse. People could no more agree to differ. All this was dismissed as mere feudal fuss about keeping forms, or as bourgeois hypocrisy for hiding vested interests. One who differed with a Leftist was either a fool who did not know his class interest, or a knave trying to curry favour with this or that feudal lord or capitalist paymaster. Everyone except the Leftists had to be somebody else's paid agent.

The swearology that followed this renunciation of reason was simply staggering, and few people could manage the manners to match it. There was no limit any more to the filthy language which Leftism could marshal at a moment's notice. This language felt fulfilled only after it had assassinated the entire character of an opponent, and made him or her look like the lowest specimen of the human race.

### INDIAN NATIONALISM NAMED AS HINDU COMMUNALISM

The language of Islamic imperialism as also that of British imperialism had been saying for a long time that Congress nationalism was nothing but Hindu communalism. The Congress had tried its best to disprove the accusation by making more and more concessions to the Muslims. Its participation in the Khilafat agitation was a generous gesture aimed at moving Muslim hearts. But all had gone in vain. Muslims had not only remained unreconciled but had become increasingly prone to frequent violence and vile vituperations. Fanaticism inherent in the ideology of Islam had turned them into a frenzied mob.

There were many freedom fighters, inside as well as outside the Congress fold, who were not happy with the pro-Muslim politics of the Congress. They held the very correct view that Hindu society constituted the nation in the ancient Hindu homeland, and that communities crystallized in this country by Islamic and Christian imperialism should give up their separatism and join the mainstream. Hindus alone had been manning the fight for freedom and making all the sacrifices for the motherland. Muslims, on the other hand, had either played the British game, or stood aloof, or come forward only to share the concessions which Hindu freedom fighters were able to wrest from the British from time to time. And this state of things was likely to last till Muslims cured themselves of the illusion that they were a race of conquerors, and that they could get almost anything by staging street riots.

The language of Leftism launched a blistering attack on these Nationalists. They were branded as "Hindu communalists who were bent upon breaking the broad national front against British imperialism by bringing in religious obscurantism and cultural chauvinism borrowed from the primitive Hindu past". The "Hindu communalists" were not only "provoking Muslim communalism" but also "serving feudalism, capitalism, and imperialism by raising narrow and sectarian issues which had no relevance to the burning national problems and which sabotaged the struggle of the toiling masses for a bit of bread and a piece of cloth". The Nationalists were thus made suspect in the eyes of the Congress which could never get over its supine stance vis-a-vis Islam and the Muslims. The suspicion has deepened in subsequent years, so much so that all Nationalists have been ostracised from the Congress fold.

In the second round, the language of Leftism accused the Congress itself of using far too many Hindu symbols and songs and ceremonies to give comfort to the "Muslim minority which was becoming increasingly conscious of its own religious and cultural identity". *Vande Mātaram*, the national song which had been the soul of the freedom movement for several decades, was subjected of special criticism as an "anti-Muslim crusade". The leader of this criticism inside the Congress was the ever-present fellow-traveller, Pandit Nehru. And an apologetic Congress was sent on a wild-goose chase after "a non-communal mode of functioning such as could satisfy the Muslim masses". The search has not yet ended.

## MUSLIMS MARCHED TOWARDS NATIONHOOD

The language of Communist imperialism had addressed itself to the "communal problem" quite early in its career in India. As early as 1922, M.N. Roy had appraised the Lucknow Pact of 1916 as a "coming together of the Hindu and the Muslim bourgeoisie in a common compact with British imperialism against the toiling masses". Later on, this language had characterised the Muslim League as a "close preserve of feudal interests in confrontation with the capitalist Congress". Still later, "the communal problem" had been explained away as a "competition for jobs between the Hindu and the Muslim petit-bourgeoisie". But all this looked like groping in the dark when the full light dawned some time later. The language of Leftism started presenting the Muslims as "poor peasantry and proletariat exploited and oppressed by Hindu landlords, moneylenders and capitalists". It was now proclaimed that the confrontation had an economic character. It was a class conflict!

The consequences were far reaching. Henceforward, Hindus were expected to hang their heads in shame. Quite a few of them did start showing a guilt complex and indulging in breast-beating. On the other hand, Muslims became armed with an unprecedented degree of self-righteousness. In the new climate, it was a privilege to be known as peasantry and proletariat. The vocal section of Muslims, particularly their press, started becoming more and more aggressive. Their cause, they said, was eminently just and it was upto the Hindus to show some fair-play.

Meanwhile, Aligarh professors and Muslim comrades in the Communist Party had come out with a new thesis about the progressive role of Islam in Indian history. Islam, in their opinion, had brought with it a "message of social equality and human brotherhood". The "cast-ridden and hierarchical Hindu society" could not absorb that message and thus free itself from a "moribund social system", mainly because "the Brahmins saw in Islam a threat to their privileges and profits". M.N. Roy endorsed this thesis in his brand new book, *The Historical Role of Islam* published in 1939. The book was pure trash. But the message was loud and clear. Islam, said Roy, had tried to complete the "social revolution" started centuries earlier by Buddhism. But, like Buddhism, Islam was also defeated by the "Brahminical reaction". He did not reveal the reasons for these repeated defeats of "progressive forces" by a "reactionary relic". Nor did anyone enquire for those reasons. The main purpose of the language of Leftism had been served by making a whipping-boy out of Brahminism.

The stage had thus been fully prepared for the climax which came in 1942-43. The Communist Party of India started quoting chapter and verse from the masters, Lenin and Stalin, in order to prove that India, like pre-revolutionary Russia was seething with a number of submerged nationalities — Andhras, Assamese, Bengalis, Gujaratis, Kannadigas, Kashmiris, Malayalis, Marathas, Oriyas, Pathans, Punjabis, Sindhis and Tamils. Each of these had a right to secede from the Indian federation and set up a sovereign state of its own. And as the people of Assam and

Bengal in the east and Punjab, Sindh and North-West Frontier Province in the west, were predominantly Muslim, they could set up a separate federation of their own and call it Pakistan. The Hindus and Sikhs in these provinces had to learn to live with their Muslim brethren with whom they "shared a common culture".

This is not the place to discuss why the Communists adopted this party line and how they collaborated actively with the British by sabotaging the Quit India Movement. Suffice it to say that a number of Communist scholars equipped the Muslim League with a lot of statistics and endless casuistry in the latter's *jihād* for Pakistan. So far the League had been strong in bluster but weak in self-confidence while pleading its case for Partition. Now it had in its arsenal a lot of ideological hardware for hurling at the "Hindu communalists". The language of Leftism had worked a miracle.

The Congress Socialists, the Forward Blocists, and some other Leftists groups and factions parted company with the Communists over the Quit India Movement and the question of Pakistan. But they continued to share with the Communists the language of Leftism so far as Islam and Indian Nationalism were concerned. The spectre of "Hindu communalism" has never ceased to haunt them. Nor has their love for Islam and Muslims suffered any loss even after all Hindu Leftists have been hounded out of the Islamic State of Pakistan. The only change that has taken place is one of nomenclature. The love for Islam and Muslims has been labelled as Secularism in the post-independence period.

# 7

# The Place of Mahatma Gandhi

The languages of British and Christian imperialism had stood fully exposed for what they were in essence by the time the Swadeshi Movement swept forward after the Partition of Bengal in 1905. The language of Islamic imperialism had revived but was not yet resounding enough to ring bells in the minds of national leaders. And the language of Communist imperialism had not yet appeared on the scene.

The last two languages came into their own by the end of the 'twenties. The freedom movement had to feel their full blast by the middle of the 'thirties. The leader who had emerged in complete command of the freedom movement by that time was Mahatma Gandhi. And his role vis-a-vis these two languages has been a matter of controversy.

Mahatma Gandhi showed the same understanding of the languages of British and Christian imperialism as had been shown earlier by the leaders of the Swadeshi Movement. There were indications in his writings and statements that he suspected the language of Communist imperialism as something sinister, though he started faltering when this language became the language of Leftism in the mouths of Pandit Nehru and the Congress Socialists. But his response to the language of Islamic imperialism was not at all what could be expected from a man of deep perceptions such as he had proved himself to be in many fields.

His failure vis-a-vis the language of Islamic imperialism can be explained in various ways. But the fact remains that this failure made the Muslims more and more aggressive and created a lot of resentment in a section of Indian Nationalists. These anti-Gandhi Nationalists have not been able to get reconciled to his role even after his death in very tragic circumstances. On the other hand, all sorts of Hindu-baiters have been invoking his name and fame to put Hindu society in the wrong.

## MAHATMA GANDHI IN HOSTILE HANDS

The Leftists had no use for Mahatma Gandhi during his lifetime They had hurled their choicest swear-words at him. But the Mahatma dead has become a great asset for them. Not that they have revised their estimate of his role in the past, or acquired any respect for him in the present. They are only using him as a stick to beat Hindu society into shame.

Muslims, too, have staged a similar *volte face.* They had opposed him tooth and nail during his lifetime. The language which their press and politicians had used for him provides a study in pornography. But after his death they have been holding him up in order to defame Hindu society. Not that they have changed their opinion about him or imbibed any of his teachings. They are only using him as a device to put Hindu society on the defensive.

The Gandhians present a very curious case. They claim to have inherited the message of the Mahatma. But the only people with whom they feel at home are Hindu-baiters. They avoid all those who are not ashamed of being Hindu or who take pride in Hindu history and heritage. They feel sure that "Hindu communalism" has been and remains India's major malady. The only point to which they never refer is that Mahatma Gandhi was a proud Hindu with a profound faith in Sanātana Dharma, and that a reawakening and rejuvenation of Hindu society was his most important preoccupation.

The Hindu-baiters highlight the fact that the Mahatma was murdered by a Hindu. But they hide the fact that it was the Hindus who had always rallied round the Mahatma, who had adored him throughout his life, who had followed him as their leader, and who had stood by him through thick and thin. It is tantamount to insinuating that Hindus have done nothing in the whole of their history except murdering the Mahatma. The only parallel is provided by the Christian churches which have known the Jews only as murderers of Jesus.

This mischievous exercise in exploiting the name of a great Hindu in order to malign Hindu society has succeeded because whatever Nationalists have come forward to lead Hindu society in the post-independence period have chosen to ignore all facets of the Mahatma's life and teaching *except* one, namely, his handling of the Muslim problem. They have meditated, one must say, rather morbidly on the one mistake he made in his life, namely, his understanding of Islam. They have never taken into account the sterling services he rendered to Hinduism and Hindu society in so many spheres. The only thing they remember with resentment is his failure in one field, namely, his inability to prevent Partition.

### TWO SIGNIFICANT FACTS

The anti-Gandhi Nationalists have never tried honestly to face the fact that it was he and not they who had stirred the minds and hearts of

Hindu masses. It was he and not they who had mobilized Hindu society to make sacrifices in the service of the motherland. Nor have the denunciations of anti-Gandhi Nationalists succeeded in doing the slightest damage to his stature. In fact, his stature has risen higher and higher with the passing of time. He continues to be cherished by Hindu masses as one of the greatest in Hindu history. Reverence for him in the world at large has also continued to grow. He is now regarded as a profound thinker on problems created by an industrial civilisation and a hedonistic culture. Hinduism has gained a good name abroad because Gandhi is known as a great Hindu.

On the other hand, it must be admitted that the failure which the Mahatma met vis-a-vis Muslims was truly of startling proportions. Hindu-Muslim unity was a goal which he had pursued with great dedication throughout his life. He had paid high tributes to Islam, its prophet, its caliphs, and its scriptures. He had espoused the cause of Khilafat in order to win Muslim hearts. He had befriended even questionable characters like Abdul Bari and the Ali Brothers because the latter enjoyed the confidence of Muslim masses. He had gone out of his way to humour Jinnah who was always cold and quite often nasty in his manners. He had ignored the invectives that were hurled at him by the Muslim press and politicians. He had even advised the British to hand over power to the Muslim League, and quit. He had always frowned at all efforts to organise Hindus in order to call the Muslim bluff. In short, his policy towards Muslims had been full of appeasement at the cost of Hindu society. But nothing had helped. Muslims had continued to grow more and more hostile.

If we put these two facts together, we can perhaps draw some worthwhile conclusions. First, it follows that Hindu society responds only to a call which is deeply religious and cultural. Anti-Gandhi Nationalists have failed to move Hindu masses because their appeal has been purely political. These Nationalists have drawn most of their inspiration from the modern West, and not from India's own great past. Secondly, there must be something very hard in the heart of Islam so that even a man of oceanic goodwill like Mahatma Gandhi failed to move it. He succeeded with the British by making them feel morally in the wrong. He succeeded with such sections of Hindu society as had nourished some grievances of their own, and tried to turn away from the freedom movement. It was only the Muslims with whom he failed miserably.

## IN JUSTICE TO MAHATMA GANDHI

There is no doubt that Mahatma Gandhi's failure vis-a-vis Muslims was great, and has had grievous consequences. But the failure can be attributed to him only in so far as he was at the helm of affairs during a critical period of Indian history. It is very doubtful if Hindu society would have been able to prevent Partition even if there had been no Mahatma Gandhi. On the other hand, there is ample evidence that Hindu society would have failed in any case. In fact, the seeds of that failure had been sown long before Mahatma Gandhi appeared on the scene.

The first thing to be done in this context is to put straight the record of the freedom movement and find out how Hindu leaders who preceded Mahatma Gandhi had functioned vis-a-vis the Muslim problem. For, although the Mahatma dominated the freedom movement for more than twenty-five years, he had appeared on the scene when thirty-five years had already passed since the founding of the Indian National Congress in 1885.

Sir Syed Ahmed Khan was the first leader to start sabre-rattling on behalf of his community. That was a year or two after the Congress came into existence. There is no evidence that any Hindu leader called his bluff at that time, or at a subsequent stage. On the other hand, there is ample evidence of how Hindu leaders tried to appease the bully. To top it all, Hindus contributed quite a lot of money towards the establishment of his Anglo-Oriental Mohammedan College at Aligarh which very soon became, and has remained ever since, the hot-bed of Islamic imperialism.. Mahatma Gandhi was nowhere near the scene at that stage.

The Swadeshi Movement was the next step in the struggle for freedom. It was immediately followed by the founding of the Muslim League. Muslims not only boycotted the movement but also let loose an orgy of riots which were particularly violent and beastly in Bengal. But there is no record of Hindu leaders coming forward to beat back the aggression. The only Hindu response to this Muslim mayhem was to hail scoundrels such as Sirajuddaulah, Hyder Ali, and Tipu Sultan as national heroes. Again, Mahatma Gandhi was not on the scene.

Then came the Lucknow Pact of 1916. Muslim leaders had made no secret that Pan-Islamic causes rather than patriotism had made them move towards a joint front with the Congress. But no Hindu leader cared to look into the motivation of Muslims. Only a slight gesture from the Muslim League was enough to elicit an enthusiastic response from the Congress. Hindu leaders conceded not only separate electorates to Muslims but also one-third representation in the Central Assembly to a less than one-fourth of the total Indian population. It was Lokamanya Tilak and not Mahatma Gandhi who was the leader of the Congress at that time.

Once the legitimacy of Pan-Islamic causes was recognised by the national leadership, it was only a short step to the Khilafat agitation. The meeting that was held on June 1, 1920, under the auspices of the Central Khilafat Committee, in order to solicit Congress support for the Sultan of Turkey, was not attended by Mahatma Gandhi alone. Leaving aside Motilal Nehru, Tej Bahadur Sapru, and Jawaharlal Nehru whose support for all Islamic causes was always a bygone conclusion, the others who sat by the side of Mahatma Gandhi in that crucial meeting were Lala Lajpat Raj, Bipin Chandra Pal, Madan Mohan Malaviya, Satyamurti, C. Rajagopalachari and C.Y. Chintamani. The proceedings of that meeting exist in cold print. Some of these Hindu leaders did oppose the proposal for a non-cooperation movement to be launched simultaneously with the Khilafat agitation. But no one pointed out that the national movement should have nothing to do with a Pan-Islamic platform, The same story was repeated at the Special Session of the Congress at Calcutta in September that year and at its Annual Session at Nagpur in December. Later on, Swami Shraddhananda was to be lionised for lambasting the British Government from the *mimbar* (pul pit) of the Jama Masjid at Delhi. He was speaking in support of the Khilafat agitation.

The Congress and the Muslim League never came together again at an all-India level after this brief period of six years which ended with the suspension of the Non-Cooperation Movement in February 1922. Muslims made no secret of their belief that they had been betrayed by Mahatma Gandhi. They let loose another orgy of riots all over the country. It was in the midst of this bloodshed and while Mahatma Gandhi was behind prison bars that Deshbandhu C.R. Das led the Bengal Provincial Congress into signing a Hindu-Muslim Pact which permitted Muslims to kill cows during their festivals but forbade Hindus from playing music before the mosques! Recruitment of Hindus in the public services in Bengal was to be stopped till Muslims filled sixty percent of the posts! It was Mahatma Gandhi alone who denounced that pact.

Justice demands that anti-Gandhi Nationalists review Hindu history vis-a-vis Islam, and lay the blame where it belongs. They will soon find out that Mahatma Gandhi was neither the first nor the last to accord the status of a religion to Islam, the dignity of a deity to Allah, the aura of an avatar to Muhammad, the sanctity of a scripture to the Quran, the holiness of saints to the sufis, the majesty of a place of worship to the mosque, and the rights of a minority to the Muslim *millat.* Most Hindus are still chanting *sarva-dharma-sama-bhāva* vis-a-vis Islam in the face of Muslim fanaticism, though nearly five decades have passed since the death of Mahatma Gandhi.

## THE MAHATMA'S FAILURE WAS A FAILURE OF HINDU SOCIETY

There is ample evidence in the Mahatma's writings that he could see quite clearly the pattern of perverse behaviour on the part of Muslims. That clear perception was at the back of his statement, repeated several times, that an average Muslim was a bully and an average Hindu a coward. But he refused to believe that this pattern was derived directly from the teachings of the Quran and the Sunnah of the Prophet.

That, however, is the story of Hindu society in its centuries-old encounter with Islam. Hindu society has always viewed Islam through the eyes of its own spiritual traditions. Islam had shown its full face to Hindu society quite early, not only in the devil-dance of its swordsmen but also in the pronouncements and prolific writings of its mullahs, sufis, and historians. But Hindu society had all along failed to draw the right conclusions. It had continued to regard Islam as a religion. The folly has persisted till the present time, particularly in what passes for a Hindu movement.

Modern Hindu and Sikh scholars have done something worse. They have presented Islam not only as a superior religion but also as a superior social system. This is obvious in hundreds of books written by them about the *nirguṇa* saints like Kabir and Nanak. These saints had the courage to question the exclusive claims of Islam while they sang in the *advaitic* tunes set by ancient Hindu spirituality. Islam had very little impact on their teachings. But modern scholars have paraded these saints as monotheists who were in revolt against the multiplicity of Hindu Gods and Goddesses, as iconoclasts who were against image-worship in Hindu temples, and as social reformers who denounced the caste system under the "influence of an equalitarian Muslim society". The saints have thus been turned into tawdry social reformers.

Falsehood can go no farther.

THE RELEVANT IN MAHATMA GANDHI

Sri Aurobindo has said in his Uttarpara Speech that India rises with the rise of Sanātana Dharma. Mahatma Gandhi proved the aptness of this observation. What is relevant in Mahatma Gandhi, therefore, is not his failure in solving the Muslim problem but his success in re-affirming the language of Sanatāna Dharma which had been revived during the Swadeshi Movement. I give below a few specimens:

"The English have taught us that we were not one nation before and that it will require centuries before we become one nation. This is without foundation. We were one nation before they came to India. One thought inspired us. Our mode of life was the same. It was because we were one nation that they were able to establish one kingdom."

(*Hind Swaraj*, chapter ix)

"I believe that the civilisation India has evolved is not to be beaten in the world. Nothing can equal the seeds sown by our ancestors. Rome went; Greece shared the same fate; the might of the Pharaohs was broken; Japan has become westernised; of China nothing can be said; but India is still, somehow or the other, sound at the foundation."

(ibid., chapter xiii)

"Hinduism is a relentless pursuit after truth and if today it has become moribund, inactive, irresponsive to growth, it is because we are fatigued. As soon as the fatigue is over, Hinduism will burst forth upon the world with a brilliance perhaps never known before."

(*Young India*, 24-4-1924)

"What the divine author of the *Mahabharata* said of his great creation is equally true of Hinduism. Whatever of substance is contained in any other religion is always to be found in Hinduism, and what is not contained in it is insubstantial or unnecessary."

(ibid., 27-9-1925)

"Hinduism is like the Ganga, pure and unsullied at its source, but taking in its course the impurities in the way. Even like the Ganga it is beneficent in its total effect. It takes a provincial form in every province, but the inner substance is retained everywhere."

(ibid., 8-4-1926)

"Our sages have taught us to learn one thing: 'As in the Self, so in the Universe.' It is not possible to scan the Universe as it is to scan the Self. Know the Self and you know the Universe."

(ibid.)

"Now when we talk of brotherhood of men, we stop there and feel that all other life is there for man to exploit for his own purposes. But Hinduism excludes all exploitation."

(ibid., 26-12-1926)

"Hinduism insists on the brotherhood of not only all mankind but of all that lives."

(*Harijan*, 28-3-1936).

Such sayings of Mahatma Gandhi about Hinduism can be multiplied. He affirmed, again and again, not only the fundamentals of Hindu spirituality but also the framework of Hindu culture and social life. He valued "the spirit behind idol-worship", and declared his determination "to defend with my life the thousands of holy temples which sanctify this land of ours". For him cow-protection was "the dearest possession of the Hindu heart", and "no one who does not believe in cow-protection can possibly be a Hindu". The sacred thread had a "deep meaning" for him because it was "the sign of the second birth, that is spiritual". He believed that *Varṇāśrama* was "inherent in human nature, and Hinduism had simply reduced it to a science". He wrote several articles in defence of the "much-maligned Brahman" and had "not a shadow of doubt" in his mind that "if Brahmanism does not revive, Hinduism must perish". There was no symbol of Sanātana Dharma which did not stir him to the depths, and which he did not trace back to its inner and eternal spirit.

And he served Hinduism not by words alone. His whole life was an uninterrupted hymn to Hinduism. He rendered many sterling services to Hindu society. He staked his life in order to free Hindu society from the stigma of untouchability. He wanted Hindus to shed fear, and be brave. By all accounts, his place should be secure in the mainstream of Indian Nationalism.

There was no lack of Hindu leaders during the Mahatma's life-time who appealed in the name of political patriotism. They left Hindu society cold and unresponsive. Nor has a purely political approach to Hindu society succeeded after the passing away of the Mahatma. The one lesson we learn from the freedom movement as a whole is that a religious and cultural awakening in Hindu society has to precede political awakening. The language of Indian Nationlism has to be the language of

Sanātana Dharma before it can challenge and defeat the various languages of imperialism. The more clearly Hindu society sees the universal truths of Hindu spirituality and culture, the more readily it will reject political ideologies masquerading as religion or promising a paradise on earth.

Mahatma Gandhi stands squarely with Maharshi Dayananda, Bankim Chandra, Swami Vivekananda, Lokamanya Tilak, and Sri Aurobindo in developing the language of Indian Nationalism. His mistake about Islam does not diminish the lustre of that language which he spoke with full faith and confidence. On the contrary, his mistake carries a message of its own.

It is amazing as well as painful that the Hindu leadership which has emerged in the post-independence period should fail singularly in learning from Mahatma Gandhi. Amazing because they are following the same line vis-a-vis Islam for which they have criticized the Mahatma rather vehemently. And painful because they show no sign of the Mahatma's commitment to the culture of Sanātana Dharma.

The present day Hindu leadership cherishes the fond belief that they can manage the Muslims in India and elsewhere by praising Islam, its prophet, and its scripture. They forget that this is exactly what the Mahatma had done, and that this is precisely the reason why he had failed. The only difference is that while the Mahatma was sincere in praising the "noble faith of Islam", the present-day Hindu leadership speaks "strategically". The strategy is not only serving Islamic imperialism but also compromising Hindu honour.

The Hindu leadership at present can be easily compared to the Maratha leadership which came to the fore after the Third Battle of Panipat (1761). Like its predecessor, it has neither knowledge nor appreciation of Hindu spiritual vision, or Hindu culture, or Hindu history, or Hindu social philosophy. Hinduism for it is no more than a political card to be played for getting into power. Hindu culture and Hindu history mean nothing to it except some catch-phrases or patriotic rhetoric for collecting crowds and securing votes. So far as Hindu social philosophy is concerned, this leadership is squarely in the company of Leftists whose slogans it espouses with greater enthusiasm and shouts more militantly than the Leftists themselves.

As had happened in the case of the Congress, Hindus are once again being taken for a ride.

# 8

# Towards the Language of Indian Nationalism

We have seen in the foregoing chapters that India's prevalent political parlance — Right and Left, Reactionary and Progressive, Revivalist and Revolutionary, Fascist and Democratic, Communal and Secular, Capitalist and Socialist, etc. — is an alien imposition imported mostly from Soviet Russia by a fifth-column of Communist imperialism. We have also seen how this language shares its basic characteristics with the language of Islamic, Christian, and British imperialism.

The salient features of the role which this parlance has played in the past have also been discussed. The details can be filled up by anyone who follows the lead. This parlance played its most perfidious role when it blackened Indian Nationalism as "Hindu communalism", and aided and abetted Islamic imperialism in consolidating on the soil of India an aggression spread over more than thirteen hundred years.

The discussion about the role of this political parlance could have been extended to the post-independence period — how this parlance has continued its campaign against Indian Nationalism and thrown the national society increasingly on the defensive; how it has converted the residues of Islamic imperialism into a "poor and persecuted minority"; how it has blamed on the "brute Hindu majority" the aggression and violence to which the "minority" has resorted more and more; how it has pressed for a socialist pattern of society till we have landed with a listless leviathan sitting on top of an atomised and impoverished and helpless mass of citizens; how it has provided protection to a Communist fifth-column which has brutalised public life with its coarse language and repeated rounds of hooliganism; how it has given rise to a corrupt politics in which personal ambition for power and pelf and not commitment to the community or the country has become the guiding principle for politicians of every hue; and how it distorted our foreign policy till all our options were closed and we became a client state of the Soviet Union for all practical purposes and a zealous champion of Arab causes. But that is too vast a canvas to be covered in a small booklet.

NEED FOR THE LANGUAGE OF NATIONALISM

The conclusion becomes inescapable that this perverse parlance will paralyse this country completely unless it is replaced by the language of Indian Nationalism. It has already transformed all sorts of traitors into patriots, and all sorts of parasites into public servants. It provides a smoke-screen behind which several types of imperialism—Islamic, Christian, Communist, and Consumerist — are stealing a march. The love of country and its tried and tested culture has been turned into a cardinal sin by the poisoned phraseology of this political parlance.

The language of Indian Nationalism has not to be invented or synthesised from a floating mass of syllables. On the contrary, this country has known the language of Nationalism since times immemorial. This language was evolved and developed and perfected in the past by a long line of seers, sages, saints, and scholars. All our immortal literature — particularly the *Veda-Vedāṅga*, the *Mahābhārata*, the *Purāṇas* and the *Dharmaśāstras* — was written in this language. India had spoken in this language to the rest of the world in her days of greatness and glory. This language has sustained the spiritual, cultural, social, and political life of India through many stormy centuries. In short, this languages has flourished and functioned in this country for so long as to make it readily available to all her people in every nook and corner of the land. No other language in the world can claim such longevity combined with such creativity.

A decline in the national *elan* has led, in course of time, to a decline in the vigour and vitality of this language. But it has retained its essential flavour even during the darkest periods of national history. It was under the banner of this language that the princes and people of India waged and won a long-drawn-out war with Islamic imperialism. It was the revival of this language which inspired the battles against British imperialism. *Vande Mātaram*, the *mūla-mantra* of this language, was not coined by Bankim Chandra Chatterji. He had inherited it from his ancestry, and passed it on to future generations. This language stirred the nation to its depths when it was spoken by Maharshi Dayananda, Swami Vivekananda, Lokamanya Tilak and Sri Aurobindo. Its last great spokesman in recent times was Mahatma Gandhi.

## BASIC NOTES OF INDIAN NATIONALISM

The *Itihāsa-Purāṇa* speaks of a people who are members of a vast family and who live in the land of Bhāratavarṣa bounded by the Himalayas and its ranges on the north, and by the sea on the east, west and south. For the *Dharmaśāstras,* which are only commentaries on the Vedic *Dharmasūtras,* Bhāratavarṣa is the field for the establishment of *Varṇāśrama-dharma.* The ancient works on *Daṇḍanīti* regard Bharatavarṣa as *Cākravārtya-kṣetra,* that is, a compact country which should be brought under one political sceptre without uprooting regional, provincial and local traditions and institutions. The basic notes of Indian Nationalism were thus sounded at the very dawn of Indian civilisation. The symphony as a whole was worked out in a wealth of later literature.

The dominant note in this symphony is that Bhāratavarṣa is the land of Sanātana Dharma. The truths of Sanātana Dharma are not convenient revelations received by a historical prophet from a hireling masquerading as Almighty God. Nor are those truths contained in or confined to a Book *(al-Kitāb).* On the contrary, the truths of Sanātana Dharma are secret in every human heart, and have always been accessible to all those who seek for them. Those truths are never in need of a *jihād* or crusade for their spread or propagation. On the contrary, those truths are self-propagating due to their own inner strength. The only defence they need is the dedication they inspire spontaneously in all those who realize and invoke them.

The starting point of Sanātana Dharma is the human self which can be explored, which can be purified progressively, and which can be transcended till it attains the highest heights of knowledge and creativity. At this summit, the Self becomes one with the Universe and sees all things, animate and inanimate, as its own symbols and sequences. In this vast vision, sanctity attaches not only to human life but to the whole of creation. This is the *summum bonum* of spiritual humanism which has always been India's message to mankind.

A second and supplementary note in the symphony of Indian Nationalism is the vast complex of culture and civilisation created and sustained by the spiritual vision of Sanātana Dharma. The base is provided by an economic infrastructure drawing its strength from *svadeshī,* that is, use of local resources for local needs and limitation of human wants *pari passu* with the preservation of natural resources and the purity of environment. The middle is constituted by social and political institutions informed by the spirit of *svabhāva, svadharma,* and *svarājya,* that is, autonomy of the family, the clan, the village and the region in accordance with the inner aspirations and the inherited traditions of each. At the apex stands a wealth of art, architecture, music, dance, drama, language and literature, all of which experiment with a variety of forms without losing the inner sense of unity. In all these economic, social, political and cultural creations, there is no insistence on a dead uniformity. Instead, a living universality accommodates and keeps in accord any number of individualities without suffering any strain. This is the true and tested universalism which India has prescribed and practised throughout the ages.

## IMPLICATIONS OF INDIAN NATIONALISM

This being the character of Indian Nationalism, certain implications can be clearly drawn.

The first implications is that Bhāratavarṣa is an indivisible whole, and that its present division into Afghanistan, Pakistan, Hindustan, and Bangladesh brought about by Islamic imperialism, must go. Islamic imperialism has alienated not only large areas from the national homeland but also significant segments of the national society. Indian Nationalism cannot and should not rest till this aggression gets vacated for good.

The second implication is that closed creeds like Islam and Christianity which are not in accord with the spirituality of Sanātana Dharma have no place in India. No quarter can be given to these creeds in the name of Secularism which they are using in order to subvert India's ancient spiritual heritage. An examination of the doctrines and histories of these creeds shows beyond a shadow of doubt that they are political ideologies of imperialism masquerading as religion. Their pretensions should be exposed, and their designs of using foreign patronage and finances to alienate more members of the national society and additional areas of the national homeland, should be defeated.

The third implication is that the systems of capitalism and socialism which are in fact variations on the same theme of centralisation, should not be permitted to pulverize India's economy, and that the Indian people should be saved from becoming helpless victims of a global industrial and commercial complex. The spirit of *svadeshī* should be revived so that our people, particularly those in the countryside, have control over their local resources, can employ their talents and enterprise for their own benefit, and prevent their environment from being eroded or poisoned.

The fourth implication is that totalitarian tendencies inherent in Communism and Consumerism should be stopped from steamrollering India's social, political and cultural life into a dead uniformity. The national genius for experimenting with a variety of social and political institutions and cultural patterns should be preserved.

The fifth implication is that a strong structure of a central state should emerge in order to preserve the national heritage and protect the national homeland without inhibiting the multiple expressions of regional, provincial, and local autonomies. In fact, this is the most important implication because the absence of a strong central state has been the bane of India's national life in the past, providing as it did many opportunities to foreign invaders for playing havoc with national society and culture.

The basic notes and their implications being clear, it should not be difficult to develop the language of Indian Nationalism such as would not only enshrine India's eternal aspirations but also challenge and defeat the several languages of imperialism which have been ruling the roost for quite some time. This language of Indian Nationalism will be in direct continuity with the language evolved during the fight for freedom against Islamic and British imperialism. But, at the same time, it will have characteristics which were either not needed in the course of that struggle, or did not get crystallized due to confusion in national perceptions.

## ECLIPSE OF THE LANGUAGE OF INDIAN NATIONALISM

There can be several explanations for why the language of Indian Nationalism suffered a steep decline after the passing away of Mahatma Gandhi. The explanation which sounds most satisfactory is that a language loses its inherent power when it fails to characterise in its own idiom the various forces operating in the field. This failure, in its turn, is occasioned when a language wanders away from its own ideological moorings, and starts wallowing in a shallow and sentimental liberalism.

The language of Indian Nationalism had become mature and self-confident by the time of the Swadeshi Movement. It was able to proclaim that the national struggle against British imperialism was a continuation of the earlier struggle against Islamic imperialism. But it failed to characterise Islam itself. Nor did it nail down the spokesmen of Islam for what they were in essence. As a result, Islam could continue to masquerade as a religion, and the residues of Islamic imperialism could continue to strut around as the scions of a conquering race.

Christianity was characterised more clearly by the language of Indian Nationalism mainly because this creed was working hand in glove with British imperialism. But here also the true character of Christianity as an independent system of imperialism was neither recognised nor proclaimed. Consequently, Christianity also continued to masquerade as a religion.

Communism did not appear on the scene till two decades after the Swadeshi Movement. But the language of Indian nationalism failed once again to characterise correctly this new imperialist ideology from the West. Instead, Communism was hailed as good in terms of its goals but bad in terms of its means. This was a big failure which bore bitter fruits in subsequent years.

The language of Indian Nationalism will have to overcome these shortcomings as it revives and surveys the national scene anew. It would have to come out with concrete characterisations, in its own idiom, of every alien and anti-national force in the field.

### THE DEVĀ SURA-SAṄGRĀMA

Sanātana Dharma views human life and the world drama as a *devā sura-saṅgrāma,* that is, a battle between the forces of light and darkness. But the battle is not defined as a battle between different sections of human society on the basis of belief or disbelief in a particular dogma. Instead, the battle is perceived as a perpetual struggle that takes place in the arena of human nature between animal appetites on the one hand and aspirations for a larger, deeper, and divinized life on the other. It is in this perspective that Sanātana Dharma classifies different doctrines into two categories. There are doctrines which are mere rationalisations of the lower in human nature and which sanction inhuman behaviour. There are doctrines which are repositories of the higher in human consciousness and uphold nobility of human character. The *Gitā* has a whole chapter, the *devāsura-sampadavibhāga-yoga*, on this particular theme. This has been and should remain the starting point for the language of Indian Nationalism.

A broad outline of the battle which is taking place at present in India's spiritual, cultural, social, and political life can be drawn as follows:

1. The spiritual traditions which constitute the commonwealth of Sanātana Dharma are the forces of light. They are struggling against forces of darkness embodied in Islam, Christianity, and Communism.
2. The complex of culture created by the spiritual traditions of Sanātana Dharma is the national culture of India. The cultures

brought in by Islam, Christianity, and Communism are imperialist impositions. Those who talk about a composite culture are either ignorant of what culture really means, or are trying to sabotage India's national culture in the service of this or that imperialism.

3. The society which cherishes the spiritual traditions of Sanātana Dharma and which has inherited the national culture of India is the national society of India. It constitutes the nation in this country. On the other hand, communities which have been crystallised by Islamic, Christian, and British imperialism are denationalised colonies left over by invaders who have departed. Those who regard the national society as only a majority community vis-a-vis minority communities and who shout slogans against "Hindu communalism" are enemies of the nation.
4. A struggle is taking place in the political arena between the forces of Indian Nationalism and the forces of alien imperialism. Leftism, even when it is not a part of the Communist movement, is by and large the political expression of a self-alienated psyche. It serves as a smoke-screen for all imperialist forces. It has to be exposed and eliminated so that imperialist forces can be seen clearly, and fought decisively.
5. It is the duty as well as the destiny of the national society in India as constituted at present to liquidate all imperialist forces at home as a first step towards liquidating them from areas which have been alienated by Islamic imperialism. The national society in India at present should reclaim all its lost children so that it becomes once again the national society in its ancient homeland of Bhāratavarṣa.

The details can be worked out till the language of Indian Nationalism becomes an effective weapon for claiming what is its own, and countering what has been imposed or smuggled in by foreign invasions.

Sanātana Dharma has a universal face. It has been developed more fully in India than anywhere else. Moreover, in Sanātana Dharma, nationalism and internationalism are not opposed; they are two necessary expressions of the same truth. Islam, Christianity and Communism are not only denationalising but also dehumanising. Their internationalism is counterfeit, and another name for subjugation to this or that imperialist metropolis. Indian Nationalism rejects them totally and outright.

# Index